THE WOMAN WITH THE OIL

Baring All and Healing
From The Inside Out

Jazmin Bailey

Published by Live Limitless Authors Academy in partnership with Farabee Publishing.

Contact Information

email: limitless@sierrarainge.com

www.sierrarainge.com

Farabee Publishing

P O Box 322, Chandler, Arizona, 85244

www.Farabeepublishing.com

Printed in the United States of America

Cover Design by Sherilyn Bennett, Camden Lane Creative Agency

Cover Photo by Joyanne Panton

ISBN: 978-1-64467-707-0

Library of Congress Number: 2018960524

Dedication

I dedicate this book to the two people who poured into me most: my parents. Linda and Julius, I am the epic result of your love, advice, prayers, financial support and Godly example.

Thank you for letting me cart around that heavy bag of library books as a kid. Sure paid off, didn't it? People are now reading my words.

Who would've thought?

Table of Contents

Introduction

"What's With The Olives?"

If you asked that question after picking up this book, you're not alone. The truth is, I've never seen so much of myself in a single piece of fruit. Over time, I was even more amazed by what the olive can produce — oil. It's used for everything!

Like the woman on the cover, that oil is *multi-faceted.*

Sure. She has glistening skin and moisturized curls, but she's also dripping with secrets; things her ex-husband swore she'd never tell.

Oil doesn't naturally occur. It's only produced under extreme weight and pressure.

Who would've known, that under that full face of makeup — a face millions of Florida TV viewers watched every morning — was a woman being threatened with words, dragged through turmoil, and shoved from standing position to the concrete?

That's the problematic part of domestic violence. You can't always tell.

The olive fruit shares a similar story. Before being transformed into that glorious oil — used for food, medicine, skincare, and even *light* — the olive is shaken and wrestled from its tree.

Reminder: People don't look like what they've been through.

When I started writing this book, I desired to give readers real-life examples of abuse. It grew into so much more, but that was the foundation. My mission was to write the words I desperately needed to read and could never find. I wanted to validate another woman's pain, even if she was never given a black eye. I wanted to dispel the lie that abuse doesn't happen to women who love God. This book has done just that. It's become the lit match, sparking a conversation most don't ever want to have about isolation and control. It's a cycle I didn't know existed until my Ex was in a jail cell.

Remember what I said about oil being light?

Centuries ago, someone had the bright idea to illuminate their journey with oil-filled lamps. Using that practice as my inspiration, I've poured everything I have — all the juicy details, all the embarrassing moments, and every painful admission — into these chapters; hoping someone is enlightened and can avoid my mistakes.

Brace yourself, I didn't use a filter.

The chapters in this book are raw and unprocessed. I promise there will be moments that make you bust out laughing, drop your jaw or even throw this book to this ground in utter disbelief. I'm not being dramatic, either. Life with my ex-husband was like a movie. It's a shame there weren't any cameras.

My Pastor encouraged me to write this book and told me the process would be *cathartic*. At the time, I didn't understand. I just kept thinking, "How will telling people all my business make me feel better?"

I started writing anyway and when I finally shared the title with my mother, her response tickled me.

"Like, olive oil?" she said. "That's interesting. Your grandmother used to pour a spoonful down our ear to cure an earache…cleared it right up!"

They were both right.

Oil heals.

The more I wrote, the more I saw — not just about my Ex (we'll reference him as such from here on out), but about myself and my decisions. It was a reckoning for all my past wounds and I believe it will be for you, too.

Even if you could never see yourself being hemmed up by your significant other, there's something in these chapters for oil to heal.

Whether taken in small doses or one big gulp, this book will tend to the symptoms of low self-esteem, fear, depression, anger, abandonment, and unforgiveness. As you read, you'll find out just how deadly each of those conditions can be, if left untreated.

This book is also for the next time a loved one *seemingly* disappears. After reading, it's possible you'll stop yourself from getting offended. Maybe, you'll think twice before sending a fiery text. Maybe you'll consider all the possible challenges they could be facing. Maybe you'll realize this person is just trying to stay alive.

Your struggle isn't your whole story.

It's been said that olive trees plant their roots so deep, you can cut the tree down to its trunk, and it will regenerate. Isn't that amazing?

The Woman With The Oil: Baring All and Healing From The Inside Out is a message for singles, those who are married, and those who are divorced, that no matter what happened or happens to you, you can grow again.

Chapter 1: Final Tea For The Little Princess

A Little Princess will always be one of my favorite movies. I mean, how could anyone forget the main character, Sara Crewe? She was rich, raised in India, and believed in the impossible!

Early in the film, her father goes off to war and sends Sara to boarding school. From the moment she arrives, the headmistress, Ms. Minchin, is no fan of Sara's popularity. Sara tells stories of fantastic times in a faraway land the rest of the girls have never visited. The tales get their senses all riled up!

When her father is declared "missing in action", Sara is left alone and without any access to her family's funds. She goes from being the richest girl in the room to scrubbing floors; all for a dusty space in the attic. It's at that moment her imagination and compassion become most important. It's the only way she can endure the hardship brought on by evil Ms. Minchin.

Now that you have an understanding of the film, I can talk about my favorite part. Following Minchin's heartless decision to withhold a day's worth of meals from Sara, the little girl envisions a decadent breakfast spread laid out for her and the other school servant, Becky.

"I don't see anything," Becky says in defeat, trying to imagine all the foods Sara keeps calling out in the candlelight.

"Believe, Becky!" Sara begs.

In an instant, the situation shifts, and Becky moans in delight at the thought of hot muffins and orange juice hitting her lips. The girls fall asleep full – without consuming a single thing.

Muffins. Hot sausages on silver platters. Orange juice in tall, crystal glasses. When the girls wake up, the entire room is filled with their *exact* order! I believe that was the first time I saw faith in action – or at least in a movie. The scene blew my mind. It was magical!

As a little girl, each time I watched the movie, that scene also left me wondering, "Why wasn't I given an orange robe as bright as the sun – and matching bejeweled slippers – to wear to a fabulous breakfast?" I wanted so badly to experience the taste and smell of Sara's attic room.

Eventually, I did. My Ex took me there. Not to New York City, but the Island of Palm Beach.

Streets from Donald Trump's Mar-a-Lago resort sits an iconic structure. President Clinton stayed there. Sofia Vergara got married there. *The Breakers* has withstood not one, but two fires, and came out "more opulent each time."

One random October weekend, my then-boyfriend told me to pack a bag. He wouldn't explain much else but that we were heading to Miami.

"Should I bring a swimsuit?" I asked.

"Sure," he replied. He was hesitant to answer that one.

"A nice dress?"

"Ummm…maybe," he said.

I was so clueless, I grabbed the most random things out of my closet — a swimsuit that didn't fit, no coverup, and sweatpants that didn't quite touch the ground to sleep in. I threw it all inside a beat-up work bag. I didn't own a nice overnighter. As we rode down I-95 South, I could sense I was unprepared. I thought, "What in the world is happening?"

We drove my car. As I recall, he made up some excuse that was likely part of his scheme to throw me off. I wouldn't suspect we were going somewhere nice.

I mean, who takes a rusting Toyota Corolla to The Breakers instead of a BMW coupe?

I knew we were several exits shy of Miami when we drove onto the island, but I didn't mind. There was so much to take in! Yachts as far as the eye could see sat on the Intracoastal. The sun was blazing. People were out walking their dogs across the elevated bridge. The palm trees even looked different. Richer. They stood taller.

As we approached the resort gates he told me to continue forward and valet.

"In this?" I squealed. My car made loud noises. As I mentioned, it was rusting on both sides from several brutal winters in Michigan and Virginia.

"Yes," he said giving me some lecture about the "car not making the man, but the man making the car."

Yeah, okay.

Once inside, we walked for what seemed like hours scoping out the grounds. Moss walls. A gigantic pot of roses at the entrance. It was so full it looked like it would burst at any moment — but the flower bomb had nothing on the ceilings!

"Look up," he said.

I was mesmerized. Each room had a different theme painted by more than seventy artists flown in from Italy. The artwork was (and still is) magnificent. Google it. You'll be amazed.

As we made our way to the rear of the resort, and subsequently, the Atlantic Ocean, he announced we'd be staying for lunch. I smiled. It was a really nice surprise.

This place that he'd shown me various times in photos had a special meaning. His uncle brought him here as a child to expose him to wealth and the possibilities of his future.

Years later, nearing the completion of his Ph.D., he was invited to speak here, in front of men who would eventually fund his vision.

Now, over lunch, I felt he was finally inviting me in.

I sat alone in the restaurant for quite some time. He said he had to use the bathroom and I didn't question him. Again, I was preoccupied with the view. The waves were crashing against the rocks just beyond the sand. The Seafood Bar inside the hotel was pretty much a glasshouse.

We ate well and after, I assumed we were on our way out, but he wanted to try something; something I was not keen on doing.

"Let me see something," he said while searching through his wallet. He started walking toward the elevators and I followed closely behind.

"I just want to see if my card from the conference will work. You think it'll work?" he asked with this mischievous look in his eye.

I could tell he wanted to get on the elevator, but we couldn't do that! I reminded him that we could get arrested. We weren't staying there! He wasn't listening, though.

Mr. Daredevil was fifty steps ahead of me and showed no signs of slowing down. Then, the elevator doors opened.

"It worked!" he shouted.

At this point, I was terrified. Why in the world were we doing this? It didn't make any sense!

"C'mon, you have to see upstairs!" he said.

When the elevator stopped, several floors up, he started running down the hall telling me this was the floor he stayed on months before during his conference.

"Yeah, over here!" he yelled.

I wasn't thrilled, so I walked slowly. A maid was cleaning the room next to where he'd stopped. All I wanted was for him to come back and walk out of the hotel with some dignity.

"Jaz! It worked!" he said, "The room is open!"

I rolled my eyes. HARD. He didn't honestly think I was going to walk in there, did he? Of course, it was open. The maid wasn't finished cleaning!

"Seriously, LET'S GO!" I scolded.

By the time I reached him, he was already inside. From my position, I could see blue-striped wallpaper and rays of sunshine beaming into the center of the room. His head was pretty much blocking everything else.

"Come in," he said.

"I can't!" I replied. "We can't do this!"

What would happen if the maid saw a young, black couple sneaking into this $500 per night room? I didn't know and I didn't want to find out.

"Just come in!" he said.

Like an idiot, I crossed the threshold of the door. I remember looking down as if I were jumping off the edge of a cliff.

Then, he opened the door wider. Sitting on the floor, beside the standing mirror, were our bags.

"We're staying for the night!" he said with this huge smile on his face.

He'd done it. He'd successfully tricked me.

He'd scared the crap out of me in the process, but I had to admit, the care he took to execute this plan was sweet. I felt so special!

"Okay, we have a little bit of time to maybe get in the water and then get back," he said looking down at his watch. "We have dinner at 8 o'clock."

The Atlantic Ocean was crisp. We rode the waves in the late afternoon sunshine, making a game out of who could best catch the motion of the water and float.

For some reason, I felt so uneasy in the water; so out of place. Maybe it was the ill-fitting swimsuit? Maybe it was the fact that I hadn't thought to bring a cover-up and he wasn't pleased with me showing so much of my body on the sand. Maybe it was the fact that despite how much I loved his carefully planned road trip, I felt I was still traveling with a stranger.

We'd only known each other for five months. We were long-distance for much of that time and now, we were swimming in the ocean on an expensive, private beach. It's possible I knew it was too soon. Something was *off*.

"I want you," I told him standing a far distance away in the water.

"Well. Come here," he said calling me over. His face was stern. He didn't smile. His invitation wasn't mean, but it wasn't welcoming either.

That moment in the water was indicative of how so many of our sexual interactions would begin. It was always so awkward. I constantly felt I needed permission to come close.

The thought of a kiss would come to mind, but then I'd stop and wonder "Is it okay? Does he want this? Will he receive me?"

I'd never taken the time to answer those questions with any other guy, but I was so unsure of his love. Despite what he'd say outwardly, I didn't know how he felt in his heart. He always seemed so indifferent.

We ate dinner by the ocean. The sun was setting as we looked through the menu. The palm trees were swaying back and forth in the breeze. I could see the horizon through the wall of windows lining the restaurant.

We were dressed to impress. Him in that darn blue suit he was wearing when we first met in church. Me in a white pencil skirt and gold peplum blouse. As I recall, he hated that skirt. It was *too tight* for him.

He stomached his disdain for it when we left the room. I watched as the actual lump in his throat slid down his esophagus. He didn't want to ruin the moment. I simply walked past him, rolling my eyes. There was nothing wrong with that skirt. It was just form-fitting. Most pencil skirts are.

That would be the last time he held his tongue about my clothes.

Minutes into dinner, he asked for my hand and walked me outside to the shore. He had a surprise. The entire restaurant clapped. They knew what was coming. I was still unsure.

I don't remember the words he said. I'm sure they were lovely. He gave me the ring we picked out at Zales the day before. We kissed and hugged. It was like a movie, but not in a good way. It all seemed scripted; a storybook engagement that was shot perfectly, at all the right angles, with the perfect location and perfect characters. We looked like we were so in love.

I always thought that this moment, a marriage proposal would send a rush of emotions through my body. I always thought I'd cry knowing I'd found "my person". My person to grocery shop with, cook for, cuddle with, build a family with, make a home—wouldn't that lead any woman to cry?

I didn't cry. I smiled, but as soon as we embraced and kissed, I was empty.

It was like a movie director was standing nearby and had yelled "annnnnnnd… scene," closing the clapperboard on our act.

When you go about something as monumental as an engagement the wrong way, your mind and heart don't know how to comprehend the magnitude of the moment.

We were already planning to get married. We picked out rings and had a date. He said he wasn't going to propose. So now, his actions seemed unnecessary.

I didn't mean to be ungrateful, but he literally scolded me for wanting a traditional proposal weeks earlier. I'd given up hope, and in my heart, I let the desire go. Did he expect me to be elated because he finally caved and gave me what I wanted?

Within seconds, his best friend was on the stairs to surprise us. They dapped each other up and embraced.

"I couldn't let my best friend get engaged so close to me and not come to celebrate!" he said.

I hugged him and said thank you for stopping by. "How's your wife?" I asked.

They both stopped and stared in my direction.

The confused expressions on their faces paralyzed me. To them, my question seemed bizarre.

"What?" his friend said. "You just got engaged!?"

Immediately, I felt self-conscious. My inner-self was screaming, "You idiot! Who asks that?"

In those days, I had a habit of forcing conversation when things got awkward.

So, when his friend arrived to tell us how happy he was and then silence settled in, I blurted out the first thing that came to mind.

I asked about his wife to be pleasant. Of course, I didn't have a vested interest in her well-being. I just immediately assumed the silence was my fault. I assumed I'd done something wrong for everyone to cease communication and I needed to fix it.

From the beginning, my Ex questioned my words. He called my pop culture references silly. He dismissed my attempts to talk about current events and if I found something funny, he often judged me and asked why I was laughing. I didn't realize how damaging this was until much later.

This moment, where both he and his best friend stared at me in disbelief felt like, yet again, I was being judged.

Now *I* had the lump in my throat. I knew I couldn't recover. So, I just stopped talking.

After dinner, we walked to the grand staircase on the wooden deck leading to the private beach. There was a full moon lighting up a path on the water, straight to our location.

"God's shining on you girl," he whispered in my ear. It sure seemed that way.

The next morning we ventured off to breakfast in *The Circle*; a room with 30-foot ceilings and fresco paintings of Renaissance landscapes.

"Rome, Monte Carlo…" I said aloud twisting my neck to make out the words.

A delicious spread of hot and cold selections – fruit, crepes, waffles, and hot sausages sat in the center if the room. A silver tea set at our table doubled as a centerpiece.

"Oh my God!" I squealed, drawing my hands to my mouth in shock. "I've seen this before! *The Little Princess!*"

He had no clue what I was talking about, but that didn't matter. At that moment, I was Sara. My faith had manifested a world-class breakfast and what I thought was a world-class guy. My guy. My person.

I wish I'd known to relish in his sweet words. I wish I'd known to make a photographic memory of the rare smile he wore at breakfast. I wouldn't be his Little Princess for much longer.

Chapter 2: Never Talk A Man Into Marrying You

"What do *you* think?" he asked.

My then-fiancé and I were sitting outside the county courthouse. We'd been there for nearly thirty minutes beating around an obvious bush. Today was the day we were supposed to get our marriage license and now, he was afraid.

I couldn't believe it. After planning a whirlwind proposal at one of the world's most premier resorts, he wasn't sure!

"I think you're scared," I fired back.

If I could *go back*, I would have never answered his question. My future self would tell the young, naive woman sitting on the bench in Florida's fall afternoon breeze to get up, go to the car, and possibly, drive off without him.

Men who want to get married, get married. Take it from me, at any point where a man shows he's having second thoughts: Do not engage. Do not coax. Do not console. Do not speak faith into his heart. That is not your role.

If men, or anyone for that matter, don't decide to get married on their own — without any influence — they'll always question if it was the right move.

My decision to call out his fear could have been perceived several ways, but I knew exactly what I was doing.

Did I softly tell him he was scared to lessen the blow? Did I massage his back as the words left my lips?

No. I did not.

I knew he was a daredevil. I knew he never backed down from a challenge. At that moment, I was being manipulative. He would take that same behavior to a whole new level throughout our nearly two-year marriage.

"You're right. Let's go," he said.

It was immediate. He didn't hesitate at all and I didn't question him. Neither of us stopped to notice the abundance of signs that surfaced the entire day:

When we shared the news of our engagement with his mom, an argument ensued. It was nasty, too. Just like my parents, his mother knew things were going way too fast.

We went to the criminal courthouse instead of the civil court. Realizing our mistake, *we* got into an argument over who was to blame for the mix-up. Then, while sitting on that bench, questioning our entire lives, he got cold feet!

I couldn't see what was happening at the moment because I was so blinded by my desire to get married. I wanted him, by any means necessary.

My desire was not set on the extravagant wedding I'd have. Truth be told, there was no wedding planned.

We had already decided to get married on a random night of the week in front of our Pastor and First Lady. My mother and father wouldn't even be present.

I simply wanted to prove everyone wrong. My pride was on fire and I desperately wanted to set all of my family and friends' doubts ablaze.

I *needed* him to comply.

I had already doused my relationship with my mom and dad in gas. I defied their warnings, went past their parental advice, and rudely told them I didn't need them to be a witness. If he backed out of this wedding, what would I say?

"He has to keep going," I thought. "That's the only way I can keep going."

By the time my Ex and I made it to the civil courthouse, we were weary. The car ride felt heavy. Each step up the ramp felt heavy. The emptying of our pockets and walking through the metal detectors…heavy. Neither of us said one word.

Minutes later, we were raising our right hands and committing to forever. We went to Smokey Bones to celebrate.

He was quiet. His shoulders cowered. I forced him to take a selfie to document the moment. I knew then, I was in trouble. He barely showed any teeth.

That empty feeling of knowing you're unwanted was something I'd have to bear every day of our marriage. The feeling sliced my throat right open. It burned every time his vibe indicated I was dead weight.

I winced, and I ground my teeth, but it never dulled the pain.

OIL POUR

This part of the story is about admitting my own mistakes. Coercing him, even in the slightest way, doesn't excuse my Ex's later behavior but it does highlight a major question: *Why did I want to get married so bad?* I believe my desires were rooted in loneliness and pure boredom. Add to that, a church environment where marriage is both indirectly and directly promoted as a goal, and you have a recipe for disaster.

To be clear, teaching marriage principles and helping singles overcome barriers for a successful relationship isn't necessarily a bad thing. However, when you're 24 and haven't narrowed down your own goals in life, it's easy to look at marriage as your "next project".

I think I was fixated on checking marriage off on my list of goals and it didn't matter how our futures would be impacted. I wasn't concerned about whether either of us would be happy. I chose to focus on his here-and-there physical displays of affection and thought it would be enough. I never even considered my emotional wants and needs. That empty feeling I described? I don't wish it on anyone.

Answer this: What makes you feel empty in a relationship? What makes you feel full?

____

____

____

Chapter 3: Married By Monday

My makeup was hanging on by a thread. That wasn't surprising. It had been on since the morning newscast. I was the type of local TV anchor who didn't let anything go to waste.

My nude patent leather pumps were scratched on all sides. My Vera Wang diamond was essentially falling off my unpolished finger. My cream tweed dress was snagged.

Cream.

Remembering the details of our wedding night feels both pitiful and hilarious at the same time. Judging by my dress color choice, maybe I always knew there'd be a wedding number two?

Even if I did, I was determined to go through with this one.

Despite my display of confidence, there was proof I was unsure. At the last minute, I desperately wanted to change our wedding location.

"Ask Pastor if we can move it to the lakefront," I begged my Ex. "Anywhere but inside the church!"

Turns out, there was no time for a change. We said our vows on a Monday night, in what is now the children's church area. The lighting was dim (my Pastor warned me of this) and only a few of my Ex's close friends were in attendance.

The friends I made during my first year in Florida weren't there. Earlier that day, my Ex told me they suddenly weren't allowed to come. Like an idiot, I listened to him.

Surely, had I extended an invitation to the girls they would've questioned my decision. They would have sequestered me for the day and asked if I was sure. Knowing the girls, they would've prayed.

Knowing how God answers their prayers, I likely wouldn't have gotten married and I wouldn't be writing this book.

The wedding didn't exactly go the way I dreamed. I had a huge smile on my face, but I didn't cry. I wasn't overly emotional. By the time it was over, I was sort of…shocked.

"That's it?" I wondered. "We're done?"

After we kissed, I stood there staring deep into my Ex' eyes. In them, I could see mistrust and suspicion. He was squinting. I was still smiling. I even whispered to ask if he was okay. That's when my smile began to diminish and the emotions flooded my soul. Uncertainty. Fear. Emptiness.

Music didn't play. There was no shouting from the crowd. No clapping. My sister wasn't wiping away tears behind me. I couldn't look out and see my parents beaming with pride.

The photographer wasn't bending over backward to get the shot he knew I'd love.

There were no flowers lining our path. There was no reception waiting for us to dance the night away. Instead, we sped off toward Smokey Bones *again*; a restaurant I introduced him to during the short time we "dated".

Why the quotation marks? Well, we met on Memorial Day and were engaged and married before Halloween. We were flying. It's no wonder we crashed.

Our celebratory dinner consisted of smoked wings, Kansas-city barbecue sauce, and grilled corn. How joyous?! Don't get me wrong. I'm down to get my hands dirty but on my wedding night? I don't think so.

Before meeting my Ex, I was used to being wined and dined at some of the top restaurants in the country. I'm talking about steakhouses with exotic drinks and rich, decadent desserts.

Smoked wings? Who was this woman I'd become? When did my standards drop to this record low?

If I learned anything from this moment, it's this: You can't remake the same old love stories with a different actor. Some people really can't play the role. They haven't gone through the necessary character development. They can't connect. They refuse to commit. They walk off set when things get rough.

By the time we licked our fingers and broke open a pack of moist toilettes, I knew something was wrong. My Ex was visibly frustrated. I thought it was the conversation at the table, which I admit, was a little *deep* for a wedding celebration.

"I'm not really a fan of T.D. Jakes," one friend confessed.

My Ex adored the gray-bearded preacher from West Virginia, so that comment sparked a small fire. Still, he seemed okay. He was irritated, but not willing to ruin the night.

As I mentioned previously, I'd become "the fixer" in our relationship. If he seemed angry, I'd ask if I'd done something wrong. If he was silent, I tried to talk more. So in this awkward environment, I did what I knew best: I tried to start up a new conversation.

"Hey, how's the farm going?" I asked one of his college friends.

WHY DID I DO THAT?!

My Ex didn't have a problem with the conversation; it was *me*. There wasn't a clever topic in the world that could change what he felt about his new wife.

Our apartment was pure darkness when we walked in from dinner. In my mind, I imagined he would whisk me off my feet and rip that tired dress from my body as fast as the wool seemed to collect lint. In reality, he had been walking several feet ahead of me ever since we parked.

Now, standing in the entryway, his steps and the clicking of his dress shoe heels severed the hollow silence in the unit. With each move, the echo seemed to shorten the distance between us, then disappear and return.

My fingers scaled the wall in an attempt to find my way through the kitchen. Eventually, the lights came on. His tie came off. I kicked off my nude heels.

I was following his cue, a trend that would remain constant throughout our marriage. He always set the tone for the day. Were we on a rocky road or was this going to be smooth sailing? It was all up to him.

As he hung up his navy-blue suit, the anger and frustration started to leak. It was word vomit he could no longer hold.

"I don't have to stay in this. I can still get out," he said from the closet. "We're not even officially married yet. I still have time!"

For the next hour, I watched in horror as this person I trusted, and thought would protect me, began to unravel. He was now pacing back and forth in front of the dresser! Something had him spooked and he was ready to run.

Except this was our wedding night. Moments before, he had kissed my knuckles confidently from the driver's seat and assured me everything would be okay. Now I wondered, "Why is he saying all of this? In fact, why is he talking at all?"

"You barely paid me any attention at the table," he complained. "You were so busy talking to everybody else!"

His voice must have trailed off or maybe I just zoned out thinking about how badly I wanted to facepalm myself for asking that question. I didn't move, though. I was paralyzed as he continued.

"AND WHY IN THE WORLD ARE YOU ASKING MY MALE FRIENDS QUESTIONS?!" he screamed.

The criticisms and accusations of flirting were coming at me so fast I couldn't keep up. He was foaming at the mouth. Spit was flying everywhere.

Apparently, in my quest to entertain everyone who'd taken the time to celebrate us, I'd forgotten about him. Apparently, I was too indecisive for his liking.

"I thought you said you liked Bishop Jakes?" he questioned.

I could barely respond before he lashed out calling me *spineless*; a trait he said he never desired in a wife.

"You're not even what I wanted," he said flaring his nostrils. "You don't even look the part."

I knew he really meant that one.

Prior to our marriage, my Ex made comments about my complexion on multiple occasions. He told me about the inner turmoil he'd experienced after meeting me.

I was darker than any woman he'd ever dated and even though he liked me, he couldn't shake this fear of being with me; a *Coolie* woman.

Coolie; a word he told me was Jamaican patois for "dark-skin."

I've since learned the term has a storied past, and in many ways can be considered derogatory.

Either way, you can understand that this man made a habit of commenting on the color of my skin.

One time, I overheard him tell his friends he had no plans on having dark-skinned children. The only problem was, he wasn't light-skinned, and neither was I.

"I do like Bishop Jakes!" I chimed in.

"No, you don't. You sway like the wind!" he said lifting his hand as if he planned to chop me in the throat.

The whole argument was ridiculous. All I could think about was the clock that kept ticking in the corner. I had to go to work in the morning and other than the few times I'd opened my mouth to hopelessly defend my actions, he was doing all the talking.

It was a stream-of-consciousness rant that left me both in tears and deeply confused. I had all these thoughts racing through my head.

"Why is he pacing?"

"Is he going to hurt me? He seems so angry."

"Maybe he's just annoyed?"

"Horny?"

"Okay, no. That's not it."

"He said he was going to leave. Like, tonight?"

"Wait, should I go?"

Had I *really* been thinking, I would've gone to my apartment. The lease wasn't even up yet.

Instead, I stayed just long enough for the demon in our bedroom to transform. In an instant, he glanced over at me standing scared in the corner and blamed his entire tirade on doubts he had going into the relationship. He said he was afraid of getting hurt again. I forgot that small detail. He'd been married before.

Seconds later, he apologized, and just like that, I forgave him and stayed.

I repeated this cycle over and over again. I chose to forgive this confusing, twisted mess of a man who would intentionally hurt me and then, hours later, buy me a bouquet of roses.

I knew something was wrong with our relationship. I knew he shouldn't talk to me the way he did. I knew he shouldn't put his hands on me. I knew our intimate moments shouldn't hurt or make me cry. I knew we had secrets he never wanted me to share. I just thought I had to keep fighting. I can't definitively say whether I thought it would get better.

Chapter 4: Panic In The Stall

There's nothing more pitiful than a woman hiding in the bathroom at work. Unfortunately, that's exactly where I was the morning after the wedding. If not for the grey, laminate countertop at the sink, I would've collapsed. It was holding all my weight.

"This audition," I sobbed while sucking in a lungful of air. "It's done well..."

My heart was beating so fast I thought it would leap from my chest. My hands, knees, and lips were shaking. Tears fell as I bent over, clenching my stomach. I was having a full-on panic attack.

"It's done well," I repeated before inhaling once more. "In Jesus' name."

The charades from the night before, the shotgun wedding, the painful sex, and waking up two hours later for work were too much to handle. Not to mention, I had just opened an email from my boss asking me to audition for an anchor job later in the day. I was *terrified.*

It was more than the job. I was afraid to go home and furious I had married such a revolting human being. All I wanted, was to do my best and finally get into a role that challenged my brain! Here was my opportunity and I wasn't ready.

I could smize with swollen eyes, but I knew I couldn't convey the emotion of the stories with a bruised heart.

I wanted to call my Dad but felt I couldn't. I knew I hurt him weeks before by saying I'd get married with or without him.

My mom? Maybe she'd understand, but then she'd pry—the way only moms know how. She'd figure out something else was wrong. She knew her child.

I aced tests, rocked auditions, and was offered jobs on-the-spot. I always exceeded expectations, and most importantly, I believed in God. She wouldn't buy a story about me being afraid or anxious. She was too smart for that and so was my sister.

I couldn't call my Pastors. It was four in the morning!

By now, I was sure my girls at the church — who were uninvited — had found out about the wedding. I'm a journalist and if there's one thing I know, news travels fast. I assured myself they'd want nothing to do with me.

So, I called *him*.

I wanted to punch my Ex in the face, but at that moment, even with clenched fists, I needed him. I needed prayer. I needed something to hold on to.

"Repeat after me," he said. "This audition is done and done well."

I followed his lead and somehow, after spending what felt like an eternity pacing back and forth in front of the stalls, I gathered enough strength to walk out of the bathroom. Minutes later, I was on TV telling millions of people in Central Florida about the perils of I-4.

The audition later that day was garbage. My boss never actually told me that, but I knew before I even walked out. I never got an email about it. No call into the office.

A month later, by the grace of God, she offered me a second chance, but I didn't know that was going to happen. My panic attack (and the epic failure of an audition) was the lowest I'd ever felt in my entire life.

Chapter 5: Tilt Your Head, Lick Your Lips

I've never minded driving. In fact, my car rides to and from work have sort of always been my place of peace. It's where I clear my head, blast trap music, and act like I'm not insane for waking up at 2 a.m. to anchor the news.

That all changed when he slipped that princess-cut diamond on my ring finger.

"Call me when the show ends," he'd say.

"Okay!" I'd respond while blushing.

During our short dating stage, his request was cute; endearing even. The guy I'd seen out of my peripheral walking into church now wanted to hear my voice. His heart jumped when my number and face popped up on his screen. He wanted to spend all of his time talking to me. The thought was riveting, but really, it was just my imagination.

The truth is, abusers, feed off control. In the beginning, they challenge their unsuspecting victims just to see how far she or he will let them go. They make calculated moves to measure the person's self-worth and confidence. Any sign of weakness and they'll be eaten like prey.

Sure, my Ex liked talking to me, but this phone call he wanted every single day was all part of his plan. He wanted to take precedence over everything and everyone in my life.

I know the intricacies of domestic abuse now, but I didn't back then. So, like clockwork, I called as soon as the show was over. Waving goodbye to everyone in the newsroom, I'd get this burst of energy when the ringing ceased.

"Good morning!" I'd cheer.

As I recall, he was often groggy. He'd struggle to respond and would quickly ask to call me later. It never bothered me as his girlfriend. After all, he'd probably been up late working on algorithms and fancy math I never quite understood.

I called, on-time, every day; as if it was my job. He knew I no longer made time for my coworkers. How could I? My microphone was barely off, and I was already reaching for my phone.

When we were dating, I made these daily phone calls in anticipation. Once we got married, I pressed *Babe* in my recent calls log, out of obligation.

Could you guess what would happen if I *forgot* to dial him?

God forbid I'd get in the car and just drive to clear my head. It's not like I'd been up since the crack of dawn or anything!

"Hey, babe!" I said walking through the grey doors of our apartment one morning.

"Hey," he dryly responded while clearing his throat.

I was determined to try and make the most of our sorry excuse for a relationship. I was always hopeful that today would be the day he turned around. So, that morning, before crossing the threshold of the bedroom door, I paused and took a deep breath. It didn't matter what person lied around the corner, I told myself I could handle it. Eyes wide open, I walked in and placed my lips onto his.

"Ugh, too hard!" he yelled.

He constantly criticized my kisses. I pressed too hard. My lips were too rough. I moved my tongue too much.

"Lick your lips," he sneered. "Okay, now. Give it another try."

I should have bitten him. I didn't, though. I followed his commands, and after, he didn't have anything nice to say.

"I thought I told you to call me when you got off work?" he said.

The audacity of this man! Sometimes, I'd try to get on his good side, sit on his lap and apologize. Other times, I could care less because sometimes you're just tired.

"Oh, my bad," I said. It was all I could offer.

He was absolutely awful. He yelled. He told me he hated me daily. He called me weird, ugly, awkward and found any way to kick me while I was down. Every time I got excited about possibly making a new friend, he'd remind me it was highly unlikely.

"*You?*" he'd say. "*Sweetie. You don't have friends.*"

He knew this was a sensitive subject for me. In addition to being thousands of miles away from each other, my family and I were on rocky terms. My college friends and I had grown apart. Plus, he'd driven a wedge between me and my Florida girls with that whole "they can't come to the wedding" foolishness. Jerk!

After a long day at work covering crashes and car fires, he demanded I make him breakfast. All while he sat at the computer making a mess of the apartment he refused to help clean.

This was my new normal.

I was a full-time housekeeper, third-shift traffic anchor, chef, and verbal punching bag.

I can count the number of times he *didn't* ask me to cook as soon as I got off work on one hand. He never made me a single meal.

Understand this: Life partners should want to serve each other, but neither should feel enslaved.

My heart was set on caring and providing for our home. I would caution anyone who doesn't want to cook or clean to think twice about marriage. Until you can afford to pay someone to perform those tasks, *someone* has to do it.

However, if either spouse expects the other to do all the work, it's ludicrous. In fact, in some of the best relationships I've observed, the work is split. One cooks and the other cleans and periodically, they may switch or complete the work together. You have to do *something.*

There was a period in time where I'd come home from work, and my entrepreneur-ex would be playing video games on the couch with empty honey bun rappers tossed all over the floor. He hadn't even bothered to shower. He probably expected me to run the water and lather the soap.

To be fair, my mother warned me of this.

"You know, you need to be careful with those entrepreneur-types," she said. "If you really think about it, they talk a good game, but they may not have anything in the immediate to show for it."

While not true for every single entrepreneur, she was right.

My Ex didn't have a real job until the final six months of our marriage. Getting him to do that was like pulling teeth.

The problem was, his fancy Ph.D. wasn't going to pay for our two shiny BMWs parked outside the apartment. My upcoming boost in salary would! Yes, something was definitely wrong with that picture. You're not crazy.

We didn't even own a home, but two weeks into our marriage, he convinced me he could afford a $130,000 BMW. The price tag didn't even seem real to me. I couldn't fathom someone *actually* buying something that cost that much.

I couldn't even calculate the payments. Of course, I'm figuratively speaking here. I couldn't calculate those payments because I wouldn't, or rather, I didn't. There were resources for that. There was wisdom. There was that feeling in my gut. I ignored all of it and just said yes.

He insisted my 2004 Corolla had to go. Don't get me wrong, I wanted a new car, but I was thinking more of a Volkswagen Beetle or a Mini Cooper.

He nixed that idea fast. His pride wouldn't allow his wife to drive such a *substandard* vehicle.

As a woman, I wanted to feel confident that no matter what, my husband was going to do whatever it took to ensure we were taken care of; whether that's working at a grocery store or driving to a corporate office. The fact that I had to beg him to get a job was a crying shame but somewhere along the way, I decided I was not going to surrender to a life of taking care of an able-bodied man.

I realize some may want to go the Biblical route before taking any action. That's cool. Pray, ask God to reach his heart where you can't. Go to counseling, schedule a meeting with your Pastors, and do the homework these individuals provide. If at the end of all those roads this man is still unwilling to work: Leave him.

Notice I said *unwilling to work*. Someone who is actively searching for a job deserves support. Otherwise, you are setting yourself up to be worked into the ground.

Twenty years later, someone will meet your husband and say, "Wow! You look great for your age!"

Meanwhile, you'll be graying, with permanent bags under your eyes, dull skin, and thinning hair.

Trust me. God forgives, even for divorce. I'm proof.

While we're on the subject of money, here's my advice: *make some* before you run off to get married. Something substantial; something you're proud to have accomplished on your own.

That won't mean six figures for everyone, but if you've spent most of your adult life scraping pennies together, there's a good chance you'll be motivated to marry — for money. You'll be motivated to marry, so someone can take care of you.

It's possible you'll be more susceptible to a charmer who can woo you with his promises, even if you can't see the fruits of his labor.

But if you're busy making your own money, you won't accept someone who isn't doing the same.

You'll be able to see that there's so much more to desire in a spouse! The money can go at any time. If it does, what will you be left with? A go-getter? A fast learner? A man who can work with his hands? You better hope so.

Contrary to popular belief, entry-level journalists are highly-underpaid.

Little did I know, six months after my awful wedding night, I was going to experience a major financial shift.

Right at the moment where things were starting to look up, I was "stuck" paying for someone else's insane car note, credit cards, and oh, that loan he still owed a former ex-girlfriend.

My heart aches thinking of all the money I wasted! But then, I remind myself, wallowing in regret would only suggest that there aren't better days ahead.

OIL POUR

There were a lot of issues discussed in this chapter — the mandatory phone calls, the lone-servant mentality, and the blind respect for "authority", are just a few. My therapist (yes, I eventually went to therapy) told me habits formed in childhood can manifest in your love life and have detrimental effects. For example: Being forced to call your parents whenever you arrive at or leave a location, never being allowed to speak during a disagreement as a teen, or having to follow any command without question.

Think about how you interacted with your parent/s and some of the rules they enforced. Write those down. How comfortable would you be if your significant other had those same requirements? How would know if a line had been crossed?

Chapter 6: One Size Too Big

As I mentioned, my Ex never really wanted to propose.

"I just don't think it takes all that," he said to me once over dinner. "You know I want to get married."

"Ummm? Yeah, but I definitely still planned on you getting on one knee," I responded.

Our mini-argument in his kitchen, weeks before we got married, was backward…but so was everything else we were doing! Talking about marriage well before we even got to know each other? Going to marriage counseling without being engaged? It was all out of order.

He was dead-set on *not* proposing and I should have walked away. He wasn't serious! He wanted the benefits of marriage but wasn't interested in publicly or privately showing any level of commitment.

Eventually, we took that trip to Zales I mentioned.

Diamonds. Solitaire. Pear-shaped. Oval. Amidst all the choices, I settled on a Vera Wang Love Collection princess cut ring.

The base was set with her signature blue sapphire — the gemstone of faithfulness and unending love. So much for that!

I adored the way it sat on my finger, though. I loved the sparkle as I twisted my hand back and forth. Except, it was several sizes too big and a rush order wouldn't make it in time for our wedding the following week.

Luckily, the saleswoman said we could take it; as long as we brought it back in tip-top shape. Then, I could exchange it for my personalized version in a much, much smaller size.

I lost count of how many times I misplaced that ring. One time, in particular, stands out in my mind.

I was desperately searching through my closet looking for something to wear to church. In those days, I really didn't have much outside of work clothes.

So, there I am on the floor, searching for a shirt or a dress…and the ring slipped off.

We were already late for service (per usual) and I only noticed the ring was missing when I went to place the keys in my car's cup holder. My BMW had a push-button start.

"My ring!" I screamed.

He was annoyed. His face said it all. I'm sure he thought, "Not again!"

I panicked and jumped out of the car. I leaped up the stairs as if someone were going to kill me if I didn't find the ring. I threw clothes in every direction inside the closet. I tore it apart four to five times. I scoured the floor with the palm of my hand and let the carpet bristles run through each of my fingers.

I couldn't find it.

He stood in the shadows and watched. He didn't help. He didn't search. He just watched…swinging his set of keys around one finger.

I was worried about the ring. I mean, clearly, we needed to turn it back in, but I remember looking up at him and fear running down my spine. The scene was so bizarre. Who just stands there in the dark…in silence?

"I just…I…I can't find it," I muttered in defeat.

I could feel the tears swelling in my eyes. It was like I was a five-year-old girl who'd lost a new set of earrings on school picture day.

She'd try desperately to find them, to prove to mom and dad that she could be trusted, but she'd fail.

Like that imaginary little girl, I wanted him to believe in me.

The attempt was useless, though. He never believed in my abilities. He always felt I had "something to learn"; something only he could teach me.

"Let's just go," he grumbled.

The car ride was silent. I had this burning sensation in my throat. What would happen from here? It wasn't my fault the ring was 8,000 sizes too big. Plus, the little contraption to make it stay on my finger was too uncomfortable to wear. Surely, I wasn't to blame for this…or was I? It was all so confusing.

By the time we arrived at church, our Pastor was already preaching. At the end of service, our First Lady asked why we were late again. I wasn't around for the question. I was typically isolated somewhere, like the bathroom — trying not to talk to people. I didn't want anyone asking, "How's married life?!"

My answer wouldn't have been pretty.

"Jaz lost her ring again," he responded. At least that's what he told me he said.

She gave us a solid rebuke for tardiness and suggested I put the ring on a chain.

"Why hadn't I thought of that?"

I rarely took constructive criticism well in those days. It just felt like another blow to my self-esteem.

"Idiot!"

That's what I kept screaming, over and over, in my head. The impact of this single word was resounding, but no one else could hear. It's like I was getting slapped in the face, again and again, with my own hand. Ever done that? Yeah. It's not fun.

Though his voice was steady, I was scolded outside the Chinese restaurant where we often bought our Sunday lunch.

"You have to be more responsible," he said. "And, maybe you do need to get a chain…also, I know it's not *your fault.*"

I was blown away. Who was this person? He was absolving me of all responsibility? What had gotten into him? He even offered his hand to pray.

As we finished asking God to lead us to the ring, he went to grab the keys. We needed to pick up our order.

That's when his eyes opened wide. He pinched his fingers tight and went deeper into the cup holder to pull out my sparkling diamond ring. There it was! He was amazed. So was I.

"My God!" he screamed. "God! You're so good," he said punching the steering wheel.

I flinched at the sound of his hand meeting the vinyl. He was loud. His hands were loud and his excitement couldn't drown out my distress.

Those were the same hands that slammed cabinets in my face whenever I brought the wrong groceries home.

"Remember, Jazmin. McIntosh Apples only."

I used to say this every time I walked into the store. My Ex would flip if I bought the Gala or Granny Smith kind. He would call me selfish and say I only thought about myself. He would throw all of the snacks I bought for my lunches against the counter and allow them to ricochet onto the floor. The noise had become this emotional trigger for me. I couldn't stand it.

His steering wheel punches also sounded like the loud bang of our front door crashing shut. He let that door slam nearly every Saturday immediately following the wedding. Of course, this was only after giving me my weekly reminder that he didn't *have to stay* in our marriage. He would be gone for hours, sometimes the entire day. I often wondered if he would ever come back.

Now, this pounding was supposed to signify something good — *supernatural*, even. He found the ring. God had done it again. I guess.

I wish I could say I jumped for joy, but I didn't. Sure, I felt a sense of relief. We weren't going to have to pay for a lost ring!

However, it was this constant mix of mistakes, arguments, trauma, pressure, and anxiety, topped with a *miracle move* from God that kept me in the relationship.

I, too, contemplated leaving the marriage, but in an environment where you're taught to believe God for the impossible, it was difficult to rationalize what seemed like quitting. I couldn't find scriptures that spoke to my exact issues. Instead, I found Christian blogs entitled, *You*

Can't Leave Your Spouse Just Because They're Mean. So, I talked myself out of it.

Plus, my Ex had to be sent from God, right? He was a terror, but every time he prayed for me or anyone else, things happened.

One time, we needed a large sum of money for the purchase of our first home. He was about to close a major business deal, but the company repeatedly said they wouldn't be able to cut a check on such short notice. He prayed and I'm not kidding, while our eyes were still closed, they called. The check was going to be ready the next day.

Then, there's my whole job situation. Following my embarrassing attempt to read on-camera *and* manage a nervous breakdown, my Ex became my prayer warrior and faith consultant. Much of the time on our knees was spent thanking God for the position I wanted. I was thrilled to know he had my back, at least in prayer. When I was finally given the second-chance audition and promoted to anchor the weekend morning show, I foolishly credited him. I felt indebted to that man.

My Ex had turned God into this very spooky experience. He also made it seem like he had a connection with Jesus that no one else could ever dream to attain. Since I was isolated from the outside world, real friends, and family, I believed his crap. It didn't matter that so much of his life didn't line up with scripture. He had proof of God showing up for him. How could I question that?

So, you must understand that while sitting in the passenger seat staring at my ring, I was once again, mesmerized by "God's power". Sadly, I didn't realize these sparkling moments were nothing compared to what God really wanted to manifest in my life. I just couldn't see beyond my reality.

At that time, I'd take anything to redeem myself from the darkness of my Ex's words, his actions, and my own shame. Every time I wondered, "God are you there?" He *seemed* to answer.

"Okay, God," I'd say gasping for breath. "I guess I have enough strength to keep going. I'll stay."

Chapter 7: We Wish You...Didn't See That (A Christmas Tragedy)

I think now is a good time to explain that my Ex was terrible with money. Yes, I know I mentioned the cars and him not being too keen on working, but it was deeper than that. According to him, we never had any money...but he was *always* spending!

New technology, multiple lunch dates with people he was "ministering to", and at one point, we were taking weekly trips to the movies. After two tickets, a bucket of overpriced popcorn (because he never saw a movie without getting a snack), candy, and a large Coke — we were just blowing money! He didn't see the problem. He'd argue my head off if I complained about his habits.

One Saturday morning, weeks before Christmas, I overheard my Ex in the living room.

"Yeah, I'm just not sure how my wife is gonna feel," he said.

He was talking to our friends, a couple he'd known for more than a decade, on the phone.

They had just invited us to go shopping at one of the Outlets. It seemed harmless to me, but my Ex was worried I'd feel a way if I couldn't ball out in the stores. We had already decided we weren't going to buy much for Christmas, but I just wanted to sift through the racks!

Looking back, that was *his* insecurity. Shiny, new BMW or not — having less than his friends, made him feel inferior.

To my surprise, he told them to pick us up!

The guys went to look around in Nike and Saks Off Fifth while the wives found a reason to stop in almost every store. We took our time and lost track of it quickly. There was just so much to catch up on, like married life, the desire for babies, faith, our careers; you name it. Could you blame me? I was cooped up in the house *all the time.* I never hung out with anyone but him.

"Oh, how cute!" I said twirling a set of mini hangers in my fingers. In my hand was a toddler-sized polka dot sweater and matching dress. "I would totally put my daughter in this!"

I was dreaming, though. I was lost in this fanciful conversation with a woman who was just months away from conceiving her first child. My Ex didn't want kids with me. He'd made it very clear.

I think being out at the stores made me feel like all of the things I desired in life were possible.

My Ex did manage to find a few dollars in the "budget" for me to spend, but I'm using an extremely loose definition. We didn't have a house budget. He just lorded over all of the money and doled out cash when he felt like doing so. When my Ex hadn't set aside any funds for me or my needs, he acted like a mad man if I bought something.

Some may be fine with this arrangement, but financial abuse is real. Anytime you don't have complete access to shared money and accounts in your relationship, there's a problem. Fearing your spouse will harm you for spending or that they'll interrogate you every time you swipe your card, is abnormal. If you constantly have to ask for cash, for even basic needs, your spouse is controlling everything you do. You are not a child. You are an equal. I wish I knew that back then.

Hours after arriving at the outlets, I hadn't bought a single thing. So, when the guys called to see if we were ready to go, my Ex wasn't happy.

"ALL THIS TIME?" he questioned angrily. I could hear him loud and clear through my friend's phone. "What has she been doing?!"

"We were…in the stores," I stuttered. "What does he mean?"

The four of us met up in the food court. It was packed with tourists, families, and parents trying their best to scratch off holiday wish lists without breaking the bank. There were so many witnesses and yet, he didn't mind acting a fool.

"HOW DO YOU NOT HAVE ANYTHING!!!??" he shouted.

Each word pierced my skin like the violent winter wind in Chicago or hell, Antarctica.

I closed my eyes, balled up my fists, and planted my feet in the ground. We were in public. It would be over soon. Right?

"GOD!" he yelled while throwing up his hands in the air. "You're such a PUSHOVER! You let her just run around to all the stores *she* wanted to shop in? You just tagged along!!?"

I'm pretty confident he called me an idiot. At some point, his friend tried to intervene.

"Bro, you can't talk to her like this," he said.

"No!" my Ex dismissed him with a stiff arm. "This is between me and my wife. She *never* speaks up for herself!"

The look on his face was smug. He wasn't interested in building me up or helping me find that voice. He couldn't stand me. I was weak. He just wanted to humiliate me, and he was doing a pretty good job.

In my peripheral, I could see our friends and the looks on their faces. Shock. I'm pretty sure her mouth was wide open. She grabbed her husband's chest; a defense mechanism from an evil she had never experienced until then.

I was the local TV news anchor essentially getting cussed out in the middle of a mall food court. I wanted him to stop yelling. I wanted us to go over into a corner and settle things. He wasn't interested in that option, though and I didn't say a word. I didn't want to trigger the hot tears weighing down my lower eyelid.

Eventually, he calmed down.

The ride home was silent, at least, until he decided to apologize. He said sorry in front of our friends. I suppose he thought that would be some sort of consolation, but I was still royally embarrassed.

We were always the emotional wreck in our married circles; bickering at the end of the dinner table or late for the movie because of an argument in the car. I was tired of it, but I accepted his apology and sunk my head into the back seat.

"I thought he was going to hit you," my friend whispered after the food court incident died down. Now, all the way home, I couldn't get her words out of my mind.

"She thought he was going to hit me in the food court?" I said to myself. "Oh, sweetie. He's *been* doing that."

Chapter 8: If Only I Were Worth…Burberry

"Take them off," he said.

"What?" I questioned.

I was so confused. As my gaze crept upward from the tip of my shoe, beyond his knees and to his eyes, I wondered, "Is he really demanding I take off my rain boots?"

"Take the boots off," he ordered. "We're not leaving until you do."

So, there we stood on either side of our apartment kitchen in a staredown.

I had no other choice but to face the bull head-on, like that bronze Fearless Girl statue in New York City. He was looking directly at me with closed fists. You could tell he was furious. It's like without saying a word, he was *daring* me to test him; daring me to take one step outside in those damn boots my college ex-boyfriend had given me.

"Whatever, let's just go," I said squeezing my skinny self past his frozen body. In doing so, my back brushed against the coolness of our gray wall in the kitchen.

He grabbed my arm.

"Take them OFF!" he scolded. He was serious. He wouldn't let go. I wasn't hurt. I was just held up. I'd seen this play out so many times before.

He yells out a command.

I'm not having it.

He raises his voice.

I grow silent.

In the stillness of the room, I make a move.

Dash for the door.

He grabs me.

His ten fingers sink into my skin.

I reach for my phone; protection.

He knocks it from my fingertips.

I try to swipe the keys off the counter.

He quickly snags them first.

Being held up was just a way of life.

"Take. THEM. OFF!"

With each word, his voice grew louder, and his body inched closer to mine. He was in my face.

"NO!" I yelled.

I squirmed as we wrestled back and forth against the barn doors leading into the laundry room, but I was determined. The idea was ridiculous. Why should I have to change my shoes?

Suddenly, he sensed he was losing and delivered a new proposition.

"I'll buy you another pair."

The words left his lips so gently I knew it was a lie. He'd never said anything so softly to me in our entire marriage…not in the bedroom, not in the shower — *not once.*

The arm twisting ceased, and he continued, "Just take those off. We'll get rid of those ones."

I paused. Silence filled the entryway to the apartment.

"Buy them," I challenged. "Then, I'll throw these away."

I remember the way my face *felt* at that moment. Of course, there was no mirror. I couldn't see my reflection, but I could feel my lips purse, my eyes squint and my nostrils slightly rise.

I wasn't stupid. I wasn't about to throw away $300.00 with no proof he'd keep his end of the bargain. The boots were old, but I'd taken care of them. To the average eye, they looked brand new.

He loosened his grip and backed away slowly.

"Okay. I was wrong," he began to apologize. "I shouldn't have said it that way."

I watched him closely; studying his movements. "What is this? Admission of guilt? Surrender? Did I…did I just win?" I wondered to myself.

"Can you please just not wear those today? I really don't like it when you wear them," he said guilt-tripping me. "I promise I'll buy you a new pair. Please, just don't wear them today."

It's that whole "tell your partner how their actions make you feel" trick. He knew he could make me the enemy if I chose to trample all over his feelings; even if the argument was his fault.

Although I wanted to be defiant, I weighed my options.

Something in me already felt victorious. I didn't care if I wore *flip-flops* that day. I was successful at backing him into a corner. He was begging *me* for something. I had power. I didn't want to abuse that power, but for a moment, I let him think I wanted to. I soaked in the feeling of seeing the roles reverse and then, I walked away to grab a pair of Nikes.

There were other times he'd see me grab the boots for work or see me slip them on to head to the grocery store. His fists would ball up. I'd look back and I could sense his jaws were clenched.

He hated them, but for as many times as he threatened to "toss them" or asked me "to throw them away," he never touched those boots.

Now, as I stare at them on my closet floor, I have to ask myself, "Why didn't I value my body, time, and dignity as much as I cherished that check pattern encasing my feet?"

I'll always wonder what would have happened if I just said no to *all* of his outrageous demands. If I would've protested, how many more battles would I have been declared the winner?

He despised those boots as much as he despised me. He never touched them, but he touched me over and over again; grabbing, pushing, and shoving as spit flew from his mouth. Without a single thought, I repeatedly chose to wear those boots in his presence. I refused to hide them in the closet. Yet, I hid myself.

Why didn't I value Jazmin as much? Likely because those boots were one of my most prized possessions. They were a status symbol in college. Now, they'd taken on new meaning.

They were a pair of shoes, put to the test in my new climate. Those boots always made me feel like a million bucks, even if my Ex thought I was a worthless penny. Like him, I didn't see Jazmin's worth.

However, I could clearly see how people responded to seeing those boots on my feet. I knew the price at which they were purchased. I knew the store; Neiman Marcus.

“Only luxury desirables come from there,” I thought.

I believed in the value, even though those boots probably cost Burberry five dollars to make. Value is however you measure it. It's the practice of calculating the benefit of a good or service.

My God.

I wish I could have seen the value I brought that man. My mere presence elevated his life. Before me, he never had an apartment on his own. He had never purchased his own furniture. His diet consisted of fast food, pizza, and Chinese takeout. I made home-cooked meals every night. I had goals. I was driven. I supported whatever he wanted to do. I really believed in him. Beauty? I had it then and still have it now. Screw him if he couldn't see it.

As people living in an extremely materialistic world, our challenge should always be to look in the closet or the driveway and ask, “Do I value this car, this dress, or this handbag more than I value myself?”

Am I just as important?

Do I handle myself with the same amount of care?

Would I fight for myself if someone tried to steal me away?

Would I sell myself for less because I'm unwilling to wait for the right bidder?

Sometimes, even when you think you have your value in check, it’s great to step back and assess.

This Jazmin? This one writing the words on this page? She would answer those questions appropriately, but back then, I just wasn't worth as much as Burberry.

Chapter 9: Jealousy and The Job

You ever look into someone's eyes and *know* they hate you? The night my Ex went to jail, I saw that hate. Maybe it was the gloss over his pupils or his furled brows? I couldn't put my finger on it, but something had me on notice. This man was seething. It's like everything went black and he wanted to kill.

The day didn't start this way. In fact, it began on a really high note. I mean, who doesn't want their boss to offer them a promotion? Well, that's exactly what happened! I was finally going to be a Monday through Friday news anchor. Goodbye, weekend mornings!

After a quick chat at the station, I skipped outside into the parking lot and called my Ex to share the news. I was so excited to tell him and my family. We were heading to my hometown, Cleveland, the next day and I just knew, my parents and my sister were going to love this!

We never made it to Ohio — at least, not both of us.

My Ex didn't answer my phone call. He was working full-time by then. So, I left him a voicemail and thanked him for his prayers. Hours later, when he called back, he genuinely sounded happy; happy for *me.*

That night, we went to a success seminar at our church. The content was amazing, and I could tell it really resonated with him. At the time, I believe my Ex was desperate for something major to happen with his business.

He needed a sign that things were moving in the right direction. I'm guessing the news I was so eager to share earlier that day pushed him over the edge.

On the way back home, he told me he was no longer going to Cleveland.

"I'm staying for the second night of the conference…and you should too," he said.

"But my parents are expecting us tomorrow," I replied.

My Ex was king of canceling plans.

He was always forcing me to forgo birthday parties, baby showers, and going-away dinners. He got a kick out of tiring me out. He would start arguments about my clothes or the venue as soon as I got dressed.

If I even dared to speak up for myself, he'd yank my arms and squeeze my wrists; forcing me to bend and do as he said. I suppose I always feared that someday his fist was coming.

I lost count of how many times I just gave up and didn't go to these events. I figured my eyes were too puffy from all my tears. Everyone would know something was wrong.

I didn't want to answer a million questions after walking in late. However, I refused to miss this tiny sliver of a Christmas vacation with my family. I didn't see them enough, to begin with.

"We need to be here…to get this *word,"* he said.

"Word" is another way of saying "sermon" or "message." That statement my Ex made was spiritual abuse. I wouldn't know that term existed until weeks later, when I was forced by the courts, to take a domestic violence workshop. Trust me: it fits.

He used scriptures and spiritual terminology against me all the time! He twisted sermons to maintain control in our relationship. He knew more Bible verses than me, so I wasn't always equipped to fight.

He knew he could make me feel guilty by weaving Jesus into any argument. It's like he was saying, "God? Or your little Christmas trip? You choose."

We argued the whole way home. I kept explaining all the reasons we needed to leave as planned and he didn't care about any of them. He had already made up his mind and wasn't budging. I was *furious.*

Why was he always ruining things for me? Life kept giving me balloons — things to celebrate, like the promotion and the upcoming holiday — and there he was, in the passenger seat plotting how to poke holes in each one! He wanted to deflate me.

I raced into the parking lot of our apartment complex, putting my BMW's engine to the test.

"Slow down!" he scolded.

I was pissed, but I wasn't going to keep arguing with him. "If he wants to stay, let him stay!" I thought.

To be honest, I was scared. What would happen in the morning if he tried to stop me from leaving? Who was going to take me to the airport? By then, I didn't have any friends. Uber? Yeah, that didn't really exist in Orlando at the time. Surely, I couldn't count on him.

I parked, hopped out of the car, and grabbed my bag.

"Are you coming?" I asked. He was sitting inside the car, barely moving. I was so irritated. Why did he have to act like a child?

"Will you just come on?" I begged. "Don't do this!"

I knew if I walked upstairs without him the argument would just continue and then, it might boil over. I wasn't trying to have a wrestling match with him or go home to Cleveland with some bruise. I just wanted to sleep.

He opened the door ever-so-slightly and slid his body into a standing position. He was moving carefully and in slow-motion, almost as if another car was beside him.

I don't remember there being one. He had space. There was nothing for him to fear.

He stood there staring at me and I stared back.

"What?" I asked.

That's the moment I took a closer look at his eyes and the scorn resting on his face. I could tell, he thought I was worthless and despicable.

"How the hell did *you* get a promotion?" he yelled while slamming the car door.

The sound was so loud I thought the window shattered. I jumped, but there wasn't enough space between us to stop his next move. Within seconds, he charged at me. I'm talking about a straight line between his body and mine.

He didn't veer. I put my hands out to stop whatever he had planned, but I was too late and too timid.

Using all of his strength, he did a modified push-up on my chest; sinking his triceps into his shoulders and in the release, I flew. He pushed me from standing position down to the concrete.

I tried to brace my fall and, in the end, only scraped my palms. My tailbone hit first, then my back and thankfully, I kept my head up by rolling to my side.

"Give me the keys!" he demanded. He was standing over me, watching me squirm, and never once offered to help me up or ask if I was okay.

"Bro, you didn't have to do that!" a voice said.

It was coming from behind me. As it turns out, one of our neighbors saw the whole thing. My Ex knew, and he was scared.

That explains why he jumped on top of me and tried to pry the keys out of my hand. He didn't care. He was willing to do anything to get away. My whole body was throbbing and now, my fingers were being crushed, twisted, and squeezed against each of the metal keychains I carried.

"Give me the keys so I can go upstairs and get my stuff!" he yelled.

I was not letting go. I feared that if I gave up, he'd try to take my car or that he'd go upstairs and grab something else to harm me with. I wasn't giving him anything. I didn't care if he broke every last one of my fingers. People were watching. He wasn't going anywhere.

I don't remember how long it took, but eventually, he let go and started to pace back and forth in front of the apartment entrance. He was waiting for someone to come downstairs, so he could get in.

"You should've given me the keys!" he complained. "You know they called the cops!"

That hadn't even dawned on me. "Police? Really?" I thought.

He wanted me to feel guilty, which was ridiculous. He pushed me down in a public place on a Thursday night. There were parties happening on the first floor. If the police came, this certainly wasn't my fault.

We stayed a good distance away from each other until, sure enough, I saw the officer's lights. I thought they would talk to him, and maybe, make him leave for the night.

I certainly didn't expect him to get hauled away in handcuffs, but he did get arrested.

He glared at me on his entire walk to the police cruiser. Yup, he totally thought this was my fault!

He had to be kidding, though. Married couples disagree all the time. That doesn't mean you go putting your hands on your partner. Plus, I never told the police a thing. In some sick way, I was still protecting him. I told the officer that I didn't make the call and we were just having an argument. He told on himself.

My Ex spent the next few nights in jail.

Eventually, I went to Cleveland. I made up some story about why I was coming alone, days later than originally planned. When I returned to Florida, he had already met with our pastors and gave me some convoluted version of their response to the situation.

So, before I even had a chance to tell them my side, he got into my mind and made me feel like they were against me.

Driving to the church, I just knew they'd shun me for even having the idea of leaving or getting a divorce. It was all based on *his words*, but it seemed so real.

When I got there, I didn't say much. I cried but didn't give them the full story. He had already brainwashed me into believing they didn't care.

I guess, in a way, I felt like I'd be letting everyone down — my Ex, my pastors, even God for wanting to get out.

Did my pastors mention divorce? Yes, but I later learned, that divorce is a choice people have to make on their own. They weren't going to make that decision for me. Judging from my choice to stay, I clearly wasn't tired enough to leave.

I wish I would've left his sorry self the night of his arrest, but I actually started to panic as soon as the cruiser drove off. He was so skilled at manipulation. That look he gave me was all it took. I knew he wouldn't be in jail forever, and I didn't want to have to live in fear. I wanted to do whatever I could to make things better for him, even if we didn't stay together.

So, I wrote a letter to the judge downplaying the entire situation. Weeks later, I told the state attorney's office that we rarely ever argued. I lied for a number of reasons:

1. The state attorney recognized me from TV. Awesome! Any chance of me being slightly truthful immediately went out the window. I was so embarrassed!
2. My Ex kept calling me when he got out of jail. He was just sucking up so I'd portray him in the best light.

"We're going to get through this together," he'd say. "Just make sure you show up! That'll look good for my case."

Ugh. It was one of many mistakes I made. I was so dumb!

I had a promotion coming my way and our lease had already ended, so I could've just moved and filed for a divorce. Instead, I stayed right where I was and I let him back into the apartment, well before the judge's order for us to live separately ever ended.

OIL POUR

Physical violence is often the most-talked-about form of domestic abuse, but what isn't discussed as often, is how we normalize this behavior as a society. I remember times where I'd go to church and hear a visiting pastor say things like, "It used to be World War III in our house!" and "For seven years, we went AT IT!"

The pastor alluded to physical elements of fights between him and his wife, and I was stunned. My Ex was sitting next to me. The entire congregation was laughing. Meanwhile, I just kept thinking, "Is he saying that it's okay for a man to put his hands on his wife? Simply because their incapable of communicating properly?"

I knew I couldn't have been the only person in attendance who had ever experienced domestic violence. I knew I couldn't have been the only one experiencing it in their current relationship. Statistics just don't support that fairytale. Why was *everyone* laughing?

How have people in your community, friends, and family talked about domestic violence? How has that shaped your view of the issue?

Chapter 10: The Idea Of Me

I think my Ex liked the *idea* of me.

In the beginning, he liked that I was smart, had a pretty face, was successful, and on TV.

But once we got married, some of those things really got under my Ex' skin. He couldn't handle it!

I am successful.

In fact, there's an opportunity for millions of people to see me on TV every day.

Sometimes, we catch each other in grocery stores, restaurants, or gas stations. Those viewers, who happen to make me highly-successful, often choose to stop and say hello. They call out to me from across the parking lot.

"Hey! You're the news lady!" one man might scream in excitement. "I've been watching you from the beginning!"

At dinner, in the middle of an epic joke, someone, a woman this time, may feel inclined to interrupt.

"I'm sorry, I just had to come over and say hello! I love seeing your hair every morning!"

My Ex would lose his mind!

One time at the movies, an older woman poked my arm in the concession line and repeated some ridiculous comment I made on-air earlier that day. At the time, my meteorologist and I made some pretty darn good TV on Saturday mornings.

"I just want you to know, I was thinking the *same* thing!" she laughed.

I laughed too. It was a moment and then, seconds later, it was ruined.

My Ex, who clearly felt overwhelmed and excluded, turned around. I thought I'd just introduce him. Then, we'd politely move on. He had other plans.

"This is my husband," I said sweetly.

"Oh, hello," said the woman while graciously shaking his hand.

I paraphrased the on-air conversation for him and it seemed he understood the joke. Then, I'm not sure what happened in his brain.

"Do you want my wife's autograph?" My Ex said releasing the woman's hand.

"Wait, what?" I thought. "What did he just say?!"

The woman was confused as well. I needed PR. Olivia Pope. Someone. Please, come do damage control! That woman did not want my autograph. News anchors and morning TV viewers are like family. Think about it, we wake up together (figuratively) every morning! An autograph? No way!

Ugh. He was trying…but too hard. Either that, or he intended to embarrass me.

All around us, people were constantly saying "She's shining. She's going places, ya know! She's a star!"

Meanwhile, there was a voice inside him constantly screaming, "Dim her light! Dim it! DIM IT!"

Chapter 11: Nomads

One oddly-brisk February morning in Florida, I got a call from my Ex as soon as I left work and I could hear the panic in his voice. He needed something.

"Are you off yet?" he asked.

My answer was the green light for his laundry-list of instructions. He wanted me to come home immediately and start packing up our apartment.

I knew this day would come, I just wasn't expecting *that day*. Our apartment complex had been allowing us to rent month-to-month as we saved up money for our first home. The other home purchase I discussed didn't work out for reasons I won't mention in this book.

So, after a nine-hour shift, I came home and stood in the middle of the living room; you know, just to take stock of the situation. This was an insane task. We had to be out by the next morning and I couldn't understand how or why. I'd never heard of a complex kicking out a tenant, who pays, without notice. Still, I followed his lead. I didn't dare ask any questions.

I started with the closets; stuffing shirts, suits, and ties into garment bags. Then, I made my way through two bedrooms, the entertainment center, and onto the kitchen cabinets. I was up all night.

Exhausted, but somehow in a boxed-up apartment, we found ourselves sitting on the bare kitchen floor side-by-side. He was silent. I was sleepy.

"You okay?" I questioned.

"Yeah," he said moving his body further away from mine.

He tried to disguise it by stretching his back against the cabinets. I wasn't dumb. The look on his face told me he was wrestling with something in his mind. Maybe it was the fact that the sun was coming up and we had no idea where we were headed next.

"A new apartment?" I thought. "We'd have to sign a lease!"

That was the conundrum. Who signs a lease when they're planning to move into a brand new, four-bedroom house? The answer is anyone with a brain, but we just weren't thinking clearly. We believed we were supposed to buy a specific type of home because our Pastor told us to do so and we felt anything outside of that purchase would be seen as "doubting God"; something we dared not do. Our minds were trapped. Instead of getting an apartment, we stayed in the Sunken Place of faith.

We never ended up buying a home, by the way. In fact, each time we even got close to closing, something random would happen. Something I couldn't explain. Later on, I decided that was God protecting me. Lord knows I wouldn't have wanted to fight that man over a piece of property.

"It's all going to work out, babe," I said.

I was trying to be there for him. I wanted him to know he wasn't alone. I was willing to ride-or-die this nomad-life with him, but he didn't even look at me. His eyes burned into the floor.

That same feeling that sent a chill down my spine the day we got our marriage license, was now rushing through my entire body. Staring at the profile of his face, I realized, we weren't in this together. I was alone.

"Easy for you to say," he finally spoke. "This isn't on you to figure out. You don't have a *wife*."

There it was. After all I'd done. Packing. Sweeping. Mopping. Supporting. He wished I wasn't there. He wanted to get rid of me. I switched positions on the floor pretending my leg was starting to cramp. Just the thought of how he said that word, "*wife,*" with such disdain was starting to make my palms sweat.

Avoid this feeling at all costs. Being unwanted in a marriage is the ultimate burn.

Hours later, he loaded all of our belongings onto a 22' truck with the help of a friend. We still had nowhere to go, and that friend just happened to have an amazing set of in-laws who agreed to let us stay with them. It was temporary, but they didn't mind, and I needed to rest.

We stayed there, living out of suitcases, for nearly a month. Then, his habit of disrespecting adults made the situation uncomfortable — for all parties involved.

I've never been homeless in my entire life but that Spring, I got a glimpse of what it might feel like. I didn't have a home to retreat to.

Work ended, and I had to decide where to go. Do I go to the mall? Do I go waste time in a nearby HomeGoods store? He forbid me from going back to our friend's in-laws. My Ex had gotten into a nasty argument with their mom days before.

So, I decided meeting up with him was the best option. We grabbed lunch and then, mental fatigue set in.

"Screw it!" I thought, moving from the chair in his office to the floor.

In my sheath dress and spring jacket, I crawled down to the carpet behind his desk and started drifting to sleep. I didn't care where I was or how it would look if someone walked in. I just needed rest.

"Do you mind if my wife comes to stay for a while?" he asked.

From the floor, I overheard him talking on the phone. It dawned on me. *He cared.* I appreciated that.

Minutes later, I was given directions to our new place to crash. We were now going to stay with another set of his close friends…and their kids.

Each morning, I tip-toed in the dark, hoping to not wake them. This was especially difficult, seeing as, almost every day, I stumped my toe on one of their toys left in the middle of the floor. It was the most uncomfortable living situation I'd ever experienced.

I know what you're thinking. "Girl, why didn't you just go get an apartment? Why didn't you leave?"

Well, I was emotionally and physically drained. I couldn't think. I had been living in survival mode for more than a year, as he ran me ragged, watched our joint accounts like a hawk to track my spending, and enforced his rules with threats. He controlled *everything*. Where we lived? That too.

One night, I really couldn't sleep. Maybe it was the fact that I'd been in the bed all day?

I was intentionally avoiding a massive party his friends were hosting. I didn't want to be around him. I remember thinking, "*If I slept my whole life away, it wouldn't even matter.*"

What a thought.

After the party ended, my Ex fell asleep fast. Lying there restless, next to the sound of his snores, I thought writing might help. So, I slipped out of bed and into the kitchen to fix myself a plate of leftovers. Then, I carved out a spot on his friends' leather couch and began to write. A blog? A book? It didn't matter.

"No one's ever going to see this," I said out loud.

The idea of having some alone time to talk to God was enough to keep the pen in my hand. My Ex always demanded that we pray together — every night and especially on the weekend.

Outside of my morning prayer time, there was rarely a moment, at home, where I could express myself fully. I had to sneak all my thoughts and desires in at 2am, before the morning show. I couldn't be too loud while praying or else he'd come storming in. If I forgot something, well, I'd just have to wait and tell Jesus about it the next day. Now, I didn't even have that. We were quarantined to one room in his friends' house.

I scribbled some uninspired words on the page, and eventually, my pen slipped softly through my fingers. I was knocked out; mouth wide-open, but in the middle of the night, something woke me up and stirred me out of my sleep. It was crawling. I swung my arm, still in a daze. I thought I might have been dreaming.

Then, I felt it move down my arm. Wait, no. Now, there was something in my hair. I wrestled with the air on the couch until it hit me, this was no dream.

"SOMETHING'S ON ME!" I screamed and kicked, falling off the couch to the floor.

My hands were shaking, and my flesh crawled. You would've thought *someone* in the house heard me. Nope. No one came.

The light from the kitchen was shining just bright enough to illuminate a side table near the couch.

A roach.

It was huge. I saw it. I felt it. I gulped.

I also saw the plate of food that may have attracted the insect to my body, but I couldn't move from that spot in the middle of the living room. Leg twitching; I knew I'd have to reach in and dispose of the food at some point.

Eventually, I found the courage and took giant leaps to the trash can. I nearly missed, thinking something might jump out at me. I was completely freaked out.

I ran in the dark, through the living room, into our bedroom, and jumped into his arms. My body was convulsing, tears were streaming onto his white T-shirt. I grabbed a chunk of the fabric and wouldn't let go.

"Jaz, C'mon!" he said situating his body under mine. I could tell I was irritating him. I could feel his eyes roll without looking.

"What's wrong?" he groaned still half-asleep. My tears did not impact him. At all.

"Something was...was CRAWLING ON ME!" I sobbed.

I just wanted someone to hold me and tell me everything was going to be okay. He did place his hand on the small of my back, but it never moved.

No up-and-down rub, no circular motion. He didn't pull me in closer. It was as if he knew what to do but simply did not want to.

"Well? That's what you get for going out there," he said. "I knew that would happen."

You know that look Simba gives Scar right after Mufasa dies in *The Lion King*? Simba's rotten uncle is trying to convince him that *he's* to blame for his father's death.

"If it weren't for you, He'd still be alive," Scar chides.

A single tear falls down Simba's adorable face. He's in distress. Something tragic has just occurred. Yet, the person who's supposed to love and console him, is accusatory, instead. I imagine that's how I looked in that bed, clinging to someone who wanted me to move. I looked pitiful.

Like the little lion cub. I put my head down and cried myself to sleep.

Chapter 12: The Art of Receiving

I spent my 27th birthday in a daze. I was fighting off a cold and had stayed up all night helping my Ex finish a PowerPoint presentation. I think I slept an hour and then went straight into work to anchor the morning news.

Hours later, I simultaneously tried to gulp down tomato soup and drive him from Orlando to Gainesville. I had to make sure he could finish preparing for his business competition.

Isn't it amazing the lengths we go to when we want something to work?

Half of us call out sick if our head hurts or there's a tiny scratch in our throat. Yet, there I was, playing chauffeur with a throbbing headache and a congested chest. I'm pretty confident he never looked up from his computer. He couldn't see my pain. He was too focused on winning.

He didn't win by the way.

I called off the next morning and was surprised to find several bags strategically placed around the *Thomas the Tank Engine* rug in the middle of our temporary master bedroom.

Poor kids. They lost their play-space…because of us.

"Ready for your gifts?" he asked.

He was a day late, but I was willing to look past that. I also couldn't help but wonder what was in those bags!

"Yeah," I yawned. "I'm ready."

"You sure?" he asked as I completed my stretch.

He wasn't being playful. He was making sure I understood his expectations. I couldn't just receive these gifts any kind of way. I couldn't just say "*thank you*" in my drowsy state. No, I needed to wake up. He expected a show. If I didn't deliver, I'd never hear the end of it.

In fact, every time he came home from a conference or work trip, he always had some trinkets to share. One time, he took it upon himself to even buy me a Bible. At the time, it was a sweet gesture. I only owned a torn copy of the King James Version. The one he purchased was written in a way that was easier to digest.

That day, when he bought me the Bible, he told me to close my eyes and I did as I was told. Then, after a long pause, and under the weight of this particularly heavy item, my hands fell fast toward my lap.

He caught some of the load on the way down, stopping me from taking a peek.

I had absolutely no idea what it was! My eyes were still pinched shut.

Before this moment, he'd made such a big deal about the gift. He kept saying, "I'm so excited for you to see it! You're going to love it!"

So, when I opened my eyes, I was slightly underwhelmed.

The Bible was very thoughtful, and I was grateful. Like I said, I needed it! I was just expecting something else — jewelry, clothes, or tickets to an event, maybe? Either way, he didn't like the look on my face and he made that very clear.

"Okay. We're going to do this again," he said taking the Bible away. He literally put it back in the bag.

"Wait, what are you doing?" I asked. "I really like it!"

I thought I hurt his feelings and a quick explanation would clear the air, but this moment was far from over.

For the next 10 minutes or so, my Ex proceeded to instruct me on the proper way to receive a gift. It was a crash-course with lessons like "How to Smile!" and "Make Sure Your Tone Fits the Occasion".

I wish I were kidding.

After his lecture was over, the Bible was still sitting in its bag. I looked down at the bag and back up toward him. "He wasn't really going to make me do this all over again, right?" I thought.

Ha! Of course, he was. Of course, he did! There's not an eye-roll in this world sufficient enough for that garbage.

"Oh my gosh!" I shouted holding out the Bible in my hands for a second time. "I really love it! Really!"

It was counterfeit joy. Sadly, he enjoyed all of this. *This* was what he wanted.

Not my voice or my high-pitched tone. No, he was thrilled to see me obey like a dog. I was Vanessa Bell Calloway in *Coming to America*; hopping on one leg because he said so.

"Yeah, that's more like it," he said.

Back in our bed, one full day into my 27th year, I snapped out of my daydream and put on my happy hat. I was about to receive my precious gifts!

"Remember, Jaz," I told myself. "Show you're grateful. Jump up and down. Whatever it is…smile."

Luckily, he bought me a new handbag and a matching wallet. Oh, and two pairs of Tory Burch flats. It was *actually* something to shout about!

Thank God.

Chapter 13: Family Matters

I didn't fully understand my Ex's sensitivity with gift-gifting until our marriage ended. Only then, did I have an opportunity to see the flaws in his familial landscape. He was starving for recognition and love. Despite numerous accomplishments, he longed for *someone* to tell him he had "done a good job."

We made the trek to his mother's house with gifts in the backseat countless times. Even if we didn't have the funds to buy anyone else a gift for Christmas or Mother's Day, he assured me, his mother was worth it.

Yeah, okay.

He was always so excited, antsy, if you will, about seeing her reaction to the new handbag, the new tablet we picked out, or the new dress we found. As I recall, she had a perfect track record for NOT meeting his expectations.

One time, I stood back and watched as she nonchalantly unwrapped her new Coach satchel. No attention to the carefully-selected pink paper. No real excitement. No smile.

"Oh," she said coldly. "How much did this cost you? I know you're cheap!"

He must have been fuming.

Even though his tone changed, he didn't lose his cool. I couldn't help but think, "Where does all that compassion go when you're with *me*?"

Later on, this moment brought so much clarity.

Why was he always so jealous of my mother allowing me to sit on her lap when we arrived in town?

Why did it bother him so much that my parents drove down to Florida and wanted to stay for a week?

A family outing to Disney? Why did he want to stay at home? Why was he such an ass on the shuttle to Magic Kingdom?

Why was he so irritated when my parents' names popped up on my phone screen several times a week?

Now…I know why.

He never had any of that. A Disney trip? He couldn't see the value. He and his mom spent time together, but that whole family thing? It was foreign to him. His brothers and sister were thousands of miles away. His cousins were in the Caribbean.

He didn't understand the importance of the unit spending time together. He was jealous and insecure.

His mother barely patted him on the shoulder to express her gratitude. Sitting on her lap? Umm, that wasn't happening!

One time, on a trip home to Cleveland, he couldn't seem to hide his irritation. My family's unconditional love was just too much for him to see.

"Why do you all treat her like a baby?" he complained.

My mother was in the middle of rubbing my back and kissing my forehead. I'm sure my weight was putting unnecessary pressure on her knees. She didn't seem to mind, though.

As I fought to hold on, she began to *pat* my back; alerting me that I needed to get up. For a second, I thought she was moved by his words, but I should've known better.

"Come here," she said softly from across the room. It was as if she already had him wrapped in her arms. To my surprise, my Ex started walking.

Then, there he was, leaning on my mother's shoulder. She rubbed his arms and his back. She swayed him from side to side.

"You're my baby, too," she whispered.

He never moved.

It's important to take note of that moment. He criticized me for receiving love because he desperately needed it. He was craving it!

These are the type of things I wish I'd taken the time to assess before marrying him.

Society hypes this idea that the majority of women are walking around empty because their fathers were missing. However, in my opinion, there isn't enough focus on men who have strained relationships with their mothers *and* their fathers.

These men often haven't had anyone deposit love, support, or care into their lives. They can typically manage in business, sports, or social settings, but meaningful relationships? That's hard. You can't withdraw from an empty account.

Maybe that's why — along with my own insecurities, pride, and diminished self-value — I was able to look past his faults.

I thought by staying, I was doing the noble thing that would make God smile. *I was the love he needed.*

I found purpose in that, but the assignment could only last so long. That job was a sweatshop and now, I was becoming the employee who contemplated moving on every day.

You know, the one who locks themselves in the bathroom and cries on their lunch break? The worker who drafts a resignation letter in their email at least once a week?

I just couldn't press send. I'd always opt for delete. Little did I know, my employer — I mean, my Ex — had something brewing that would force me to pack up my things and go.

OIL POUR

As I recall, my Ex's family and I had many differences beyond what I discussed in this chapter. At first, it was an exciting aspect of my new life. I was ready and willing to embrace his culture, food, and traditions — and I did. I had an interest in his history, even though he squawked about the idea of visiting my only living grandparent in Alabama. "*I'll never go there,*" he said.

Mostly due to my work schedule, I agreed to spend every major holiday with his family. I smiled, though annoyed, as we spoke in cliché church sayings at the dinner table. There was very little life in the room. The energy was dead. Other than the clicking of forks hitting our plates, the only other sound was...silence.

To be fair, this is all coming from someone with a dozen uncles and aunts. I have cousins galore and family dinners have never lacked *energy*. It just wasn't what I was used to. So many are blindsided by this predicament in marriage. In every sense, the polarity of our individual upbringings did more to separate us than bring us together.

What are you looking for in an extended family? In-laws?

What questions about your significant other's family (future or present) do you want to be answered?

Chapter 14: The Ultimate Con

I knew I shouldn't do it. I was squirming in my chair; tossing and turning with each question that came across the desk.

"I just need you to sign a few papers and we should be all set," the car salesmen said.

He knew. I knew. Everybody knew — this was a BAD deal.

Days before this embarrassing moment at the BMW dealership, I got a phone call in the middle of the night.

"Jaz, I'm so sorry to wake you," he said.

It was like 12:30 in the morning. My Ex knew I had to wake up in less than two hours for work. I wanted to scream! There was no way I'd fall back asleep!

"What's up?" I asked. I was groggy but listening.

He told me his mom was in a car accident. My heart sank for a second. I was unsure of how this phone call would end. What if she didn't survive?

"My mom is fine," he assured me.

I breathed a huge sigh of relief and then, I got that feeling; a gut feeling that we didn't need to be on the phone. Something told me the words coming out of his mouth weren't to be trusted. He didn't sound sad or in shock. I sensed deceit in his voice.

"I'm happy to hear she's okay," I said.

He went on to tell the story of God's grace and protection, and how his mother was miraculously saved. Then, he dropped the bomb I was waiting for.

"So, her car is totaled. She doesn't have anything to drive. Do you think we could give her your car for a little bit?"

In exchange, he said I would get *his* BMW and he would drive his old car.

I agreed.

That's what family does, right? I would've wanted the same help for my mother or father. Plus, I was mentally exhausted. I didn't have the energy to fight him.

So, that settled it. My baby — the BMW I picked off the showroom floor — was heading to his mother's driveway.

Two hours north of her home, my Ex and I were now subletting a moldy apartment with bad air circulation. My roach encounter motivated him to find us a more permanent place to stay, but I wasn't happy with the arrangement.

Our belongings were scattered across three separate locations. Our mail was being directed to a friend's house. We cooked in aluminum pans and had just the bare necessities hanging in our closet. For a while, more than half of my wardrobe was stuffed in a POD, miles away. This was no way for a woman to live.

On top of my disorganized reality, I couldn't stop reliving the haunting details of a domestic shooting I covered at work.

It was the story of a man who'd violently abused his wife, stabbed her, and then ran her over outside her job. The sheriff told us the husband later killed himself and their kids on Interstate 4.

"My husband has a gun," was a thought that often pierced my brain.

I'd shrug and move on, but the thought would always come back. I just didn't feel safe and when you don't feel safe, it's hard to make sound decisions.

"So, I have an idea," he said a few days after making that late-night phone call.

"Okay, what is it?" I asked, chewing my last bite of dinner.

"It's Mother's Day and I know we were planning on giving my mom your car until she figures something out, but I really don't want to give her something *old* as a gift."

I didn't like where this was going. Old? My car was a 2014 BMW 428i Gran Coupe. The first of its class. It was spectacular!

"My car isn't old," I said, questioning his intentions.

"Well, you know what I mean —something someone else has been driving. I want to give her something *nice*!"

To my surprise, he'd already found a used BMW for his mom. To get it, all we'd have to do is trade in my car. It was such a splendid plan! Obviously, I'm being sarcastic. It was beyond stupid!

Who trades in a perfectly good car that you still owe money on, for a used car? Why? Why couldn't she just drive my car until she got back on her feet?

In the days following his mother's accident, my Ex spent an excessive amount of time at the dealership. He was working out all the kinks in his plan, without me. His trips to BMW weren't exactly rare, though. So, I didn't question him. He was constantly getting his car washed or test-driving something else. He *loved* cars.

I felt confident he wasn't buying anything when he stopped there. Plus, think about it. If my Ex was at BMW, he wasn't at home causing a scene. I needed that break. The stress of the relationship was really starting to get to me.

I wasn't waking up on time for work. When I did get there, I couldn't smile and hide my misery. I was cracking. Whenever someone asked, I blamed my disheveled look on lack of sleep. I simply was not taking care of myself.

These are just some of the recognizable signs of abuse. At least, that's what domestic violence advocates told me in interviews I conducted on live TV.

Each time a local woman was killed at the hands of her husband or boyfriend, I was thrust into an unsettling position. It was my duty to bring awareness to the prevalent issues in our community, but the answers to my carefully-posed questions made me paranoid. I had a vested interest in the topic. I wanted to know how to protect myself and I was seeking validation to leave. However, I'd often have to remind myself to disengage. I didn't want anyone to catch on. It was so difficult, though. The women these experts were describing, the behaviors they listed — it was all *me.*

Back at the dinner table, my Ex continued his sales pitch. Skepticism rested on my face, but my Ex came prepared. He had an answer to every single question.

"You know my mom's credit likely won't allow her to get a new car. It's just not possible," he explained. "If we do this, then she'd be able to pay for half of the monthly payments *and* make a down payment."

A note to whoever may need to hear this: Anyone and I repeat *anyone*, can get a car. Credit is not a barrier. It may not be the car that person wants and the interest rate may not be the best, but they can certainly drive off someone's lot in a new set of wheels, especially if they have a down payment. Don't ever fall for that crap.

I wasn't thinking, though. By the end of the conversation, I agreed to the dumbest thing I could've ever done. I gave away my baby — the first car I ever really loved — for nothing!

The day of the trade-in, the paperwork at BMW came back fast. My heart was racing. I kept thinking, "I should call my Dad. I should call my Dad!"

Do you think I called? No. All the intuition in the world couldn't stop what was happening.

The salesman asked a question, but I couldn't make out what he was saying. I needed to snap out of it!

"Oh, we'll both be on it," my Ex said. Then, I knew I was screwed.

I went from having my own car, which I loved, with the perfect seat color and perfect feel, to being the *co-owner* of a certified granny-mobile; a 5Series burgundy nightmare that I wouldn't even be driving!

We dropped the car off over Mother's Day weekend. My mom likely got a card and a dress, or a bottle of perfume. His mom got a whole freaking car at my expense! Weeks later, and by weeks, I mean like two, my Ex and I got into the argument of a lifetime. I'd seemingly done the nicest thing I could do for his family and he couldn't find the adequate space in his heart to give me a freaking break.

His mom had driven up to see us in the car we bought her and even came to church with us. The day, by most definitions, was an absolute win. Mom was happy. We were happy. Now, we just had to find something to eat.

The three of us settled on McDonald's because his mom needed to get back down South. I had my phone in my hand, typing a Facebook post about the amazing message at church. His mom even agreed with me as I read the post out loud. What we couldn't see, was the fury building within my Ex's chest.

"YOU ARE SO INCREDIBLY RUDE!" he yelled at the top of his lungs. Here he was, once again, bashing the steering wheel.

"What?" I questioned. "What are you talking about?"

From the back seat, his mother begged for him to calm down, but he wouldn't listen. He shut her down quickly.

"No, mom!" he shouted. "She can't even have a decent conversation with people because she's so worried about putting stuff on *Facebook*!"

I now had that piercing feeling in my throat. I knew it well. It ached. I hated feeling misunderstood. I hated that he always made me look bad in front of other people. So what, if I was on my phone? I wasn't his child. Plus, he certainly didn't need to pound the steering wheel to prove his point.

I had so much joy when we left church. I just wanted other people to hear what my Pastor shared. It helped me. Didn't he understand that by posting it, someone else might get the same help they needed?

No. He did not.

The situation fizzled in minutes as our wait in the drive-thru came to an end. When he pleasantly thanked the workers for our food, I shrugged and thought to myself, "maybe he was just hungry. If not, he needs to get a grip on life."

We were all silent in the car eating McNuggets and fries until his mother gave a shocking admission.

"You cannot talk to your wife like this," she said.

He tried to interrupt, but she was firm.

"No, let me finish. It's important you get this right," she said.

"You can't allow your boys, when you two have kids, to see you talking to their mom like this…I know where you get it from. *Me.*"

My eyes grew wide. My last McNugget slipped from my grasp. It was all starting to make sense. He was acting out — or at least taking out — all of his frustrations from growing up in her household — *on me.*

"I know I was hard on you and I got angry sometimes and I yelled, but you can't do this to Jazmin. You can't," she said.

He agreed and apologized.

Later, as she drove off toward the freeway, I could feel the tension coming from the driver's seat. He was still angry.

He never liked correction. Let's be real, who does? But this guy? He definitely struggled with it. Any moment of rebuke was almost immediately followed by his rebellion.

He'd do the *exact thing* our Pastor, his mom, or other husbands told him not to do. He was defiant and unwilling to change.

He said something rude as we parked. I don't remember the words, but they were enough to start another argument. Then, the aching returned.

My throat was sore trying to shout over his assaults on my character. At that very moment, I decided I had enough for the day. I just didn't have the strength to listen to his crap anymore.

When he got out of the car, I walked around as if I was going into the apartment, but then, made a quick-turn for the driver's side door. The fact that I even thought to pretend should have been an indication that I wasn't safe. I often made escape plans — but never actually carried them out.

By the time I got in the driver's seat, he was on to me. He grabbed the car door and then, my arm. He pulled with all his strength, dragging about a quarter of my body toward the scorching hot cement. I could feel the heat coming from the engine.

"Let me go!" I cried.

I couldn't stop the tears now. I was emotionally and physically defeated. I felt like I was about to break. He let go and as I sat up, it took a couple seconds for me to just catch my breath.

"Where are you going, huh?" he asked. "Hey! Look at me. Tell me...where are you going?"

He was taunting me.

"I don't know. I just need to go...*think* for a second," I sobbed. "I'll just go to the park or something."

"Oh okay," he said. His body briefly rose from the driver's side window but quickly returned.

"So, Ummm...how are you gonna go?" he asked. "How are you getting there?"

I turned with my entire face scrunched. I was baffled.

"What?" I said as tears rolled down my face.

"How. Are. You. Getting. There?" he said slowly, enunciating each word.

"I'm taking my car...I'm just going to the park," I said wiping away the tears.

He was silent; silent because he knew he was about to send my entire world crashing down. All it took was eight words.

He leaned in close, placing his head through the window just beyond the door handle. I had my head down. I just wanted him to say whatever he needed to and let me go. I didn't have time for an apology or for him to try and explain his ridiculous actions.

I just kept thinking, "Let him talk, Jazmin. Let him talk."

He got closer. I could feel his breath.

"S*weetie, you don't have a car, remember?*"

I gasped but there was no sound; like someone had stolen all of my air. My head swung up and turned to meet his face.

The phone call, the favor, the bad deal at BMW; it was all leading up to this moment. He couldn't wait to reveal to me that I didn't own a car and that I had no way to escape.

I thought, "He *planned* that...and that's terrifying."

Chapter 15: One More Night

"Where are the keys?!" he asked. The force behind those words matched his violent tug on the door handle.

"Oh. Ummm," I said fondling through my purse. "I must have left the —"

I hadn't even finished my sentence and he was already storming off, throwing his hands in the air.

"This BITCH!" he hissed, making his way toward the movie theater.

It was an angry whisper, but I'm glad I heard it. At that exact moment, I slowed my pace. I wasn't going to run or speed-walk. I knew exactly where the keys were.

Clearly, they'd fallen from the cup holder to the floor during our movie. There was no reason for him to call me out of my name. Either someone found them and turned them in, or they were sitting right on the floor where we left them.

"Hey! Hey! Are these yours?"

A guy flagged me down as I made my way past the concession stand. "We were looking for you, but you guys ran out so fast," he said.

"Thank you," I said handing the keys over to my Ex.

He knew he should calm down, but he didn't want to. He was holding on to his anger because I made another mistake; something he didn't allow in our house, at least not from me.

On our way home, I tried several times to break the silence. My Ex was determined to ignore me and ride without any sound, except for the roar of the engine.

"Oh, look! My Dad called me," I said out loud.

Everybody knows, checking your phone is one of the best ways to pass the time when things get awkward. When my Ex decided not to answer, I called my father back.

Part of me believed my Ex might try to harm me. So, yes — this call was also me going into survival mode. He was flying down the road in a BMW, weaving in and out of traffic. I knew he wouldn't get too stupid with my Dad on the phone.

"My Dad says hi," I told him. He didn't respond.

My Ex didn't care to make a good impression in front of my Dad or any of my family for that matter. He was utterly disrespectful.

On the call, my father could sense the anxiety in my voice. He knew my Ex and I were at odds, but simply told me to call him in the morning. To me, his words that night sounded like a faith declaration. It was like my Dad was holding out hope that he'd hear my voice again.

Those are the moments I wish I could erase; moments where my parents had to fight the evil thought that their beautiful daughter wouldn't make it to *see* the next day. It's a difficulty no parent should have to face.

He parked. We went inside the apartment. I sat down at the computer and within seconds, he grabbed the keys, walked out, and let the door slam shut behind him.

"What a big baby!" I thought. He had nothing to be angry about. I rolled my eyes and continued to scroll through Pinterest.

"Let me find a picture of *Oprah,"* I thought to myself.

Before our movie date, I'd been putting together a vision board. This was seemingly my darkest moment and yet, I was compiling pictures of the dream life I wanted to see: a Range Rover, a Louis Vuitton handbag, a vacation to Greece, Oprah — those were the anchors I tied to my success. They were all basic-level aspirations, but at the time, seeing them on my screen kept me sane. These were my goals; not the toxic life I was currently living. I just had to keep going. I couldn't let him kill me. I couldn't let him kill my dreams.

When he returned 30 minutes later, I barely lifted my eyes from the screen. Slowly, he shut the door and massaged the lock with his finger.

"I'm sorry," he said blankly. Then, while clearing his throat, he confirmed my worst fear.

"I just get so angry with you," he explained. "When I drove off, I was trying to figure out why I was so mad."

This conversation piqued my interest. I tilted my head. Had he finally come to his senses?

Was this the moment where he broke down and surrendered? I was all ears.

"I realized, you don't even have to do anything. I just become *enraged*…by you," he said.

I'm pretty sure my jaw dropped. I picked it up quickly, but my body was in full shock.

I thought, "Oh my God. Did he just say what I think he said?!"

He apologized and told me he was going to lay down for the night. I didn't move.

"I think it's time for me to go," I whispered into the empty living room.

You ever know a change is imminent? You can feel it? Taste it? Deep within, you just know *something* is going to be different?

Yeah, this was it.

Chapter 16: The Day I Left

I woke up to the sound of birds chirping on our outdoor balcony. The sun was blazing, and nothing could deflect its brilliance. After all, we didn't have much furniture in the apartment.

"Alright," he said letting out a deep sigh. "Let's pray."

Praying together on weekend mornings was an especially excruciating task. My Ex was so long-winded! He just went on and on, telling God how much he loved Him. I'd sit there thinking to myself, "Alright. We get it!"

That morning, I wasn't in the mood to argue. I simply hoped he would be brief.

We were up early to volunteer at a children's camp. He was so passionate about speaking to the kids there, he forced me to come along with him. He even recruited one of his friends to help.

That friend just happened to have a baby on the way, and after the event, we decided to give him and his wife a break. My Ex and I took their two oldest kids home with us.

So, let's recap for a second, shall we? After a long week at work, I was yelled at after a movie and stormed out on a Friday night.

I woke up early to volunteer with kids Saturday morning and then, brought two kids home to babysit. I was pooped! Apparently, my Ex was not.

"What do you want to do tonight?" He asked.

The girls were on the floor playing with a few of their toys. I had already fed them, and it was about time for us to meet with their parents. As we waited, I pulled out my phone to type a work email that I forgot to send earlier in the day. I barely looked up at my Ex to answer.

"I don't want to do anything," I explained. "I'm tired."

He didn't respond. He just sat there quietly on the opposite side of our sectional and stared at the ground. I noticed and thought his reaction was odd, but I ignored him. I went back to my email. Minutes passed as I tried to condense the sentences.

"Jaz!" he called still keeping his gaze on the ground. I could see him in my peripheral vision. Why was he being so strange?

"Yes?" I answered.

"Can you put the phone down and answer me?!" he demanded.

Here we were again. I was being yelled at, like a child, for playing with my phone. Only, I wasn't playing.

To oblige him, I placed the phone on my lap and stared directly into his face.

"What do you want *to do*?" he asked again.

He put extra emphasis on those last two words. My Ex clearly wanted an answer, which was odd, because I thought I'd already given him one.

"I don't want to go anywhere," I explained. "We've been running around with kids *all day*."

In frustration, I rolled my eyes and picked up my phone again. What more did he want? I answered, didn't I?

Within seconds, I watched out of the corner of my eye, as he lunged forward and thrust his entire body into mine; pushing me backward into the couch. Then, he formed his left hand into a blade, leaving no space between any finger, and chopped me in my throat.

The girls gasped behind the couch.

I glared at him as he stood over me. My eyes were stretched to their limits and my chest was rising and falling faster than God ever designed it to do so. *He hit me. Again.*

"What is wrong with you!" I screamed.

I couldn't believe it. He put his hands on me…in front of the kids?

I realized then, he didn't give a damn. I couldn't stay. I couldn't let my story end with me hitting my head on a sink or a wall. I was too good for that. There was too much inside of me. Too many people had fought to make sure I made it. I couldn't let him kill me.

In the time it took me to get my bearings, he grabbed my phone and the set of keys I'd been using. Both were collateral.

"Give me my keys!" I said shaking.

"Let's just go drop off the girls," he said. "Then, me and you can *talk*."

I didn't believe him. I looked into his eyes and something told me, I wouldn't make it out alive if I got into a car with him.

I was standing in an apartment with no car to my name, no phone in my possession and a person intent on hurting me blocking the door. My mind raced. "Do I run past him just to get outside? Do I fight him for my phone?"

"Girls, get your stuff together," he instructed.

I can't remember exactly what happened after that. I think I had an epiphany that his set of keys to the old car were in my purse.

It wasn't ideal, but I was okay with driving off in that rundown piece of crap. I wasn't going to fight over a silly car. I just needed to get my phone back.

Fortunately, when I told him I'd go on this ride to drop off the girls, he forked it over. Thank God.

As we walked outside, I kept the girls close. I wasn't sure what he would do. However, there were three flights of stairs ahead of us and I didn't trust him. This man had been going off for months; openly expressing his inability to control his anger.

Plus, he had just knocked the air out of my lungs. In that moment on the couch, he pushed me so hard I legitimately thought my body was going to flip over.

As the girls crawled into the backseat, I reached into my purse and grabbed the other set of keys. I made sure I had a firm grip on the keyring. When I looked up from my bag, he was staring at me. He wanted me to get inside.

"I can't in my right mind get in this car with you," I said.

I didn't even recognize my voice. It was strong. It was certain. It was well-thought out; something my thoughts hadn't been in years.

I could tell he was confused. He didn't understand what I was saying.

His two cars were parked side-by-side and I simply decided to turn, open the door to the older one and get inside.

"What are you doing?!" he asked running over to the driver's side window.

I panicked. I didn't want to roll the window down. I was willing to pull off and drive over his feet if I had to! Through a small crack in a glass, I explained myself for a second time. I wasn't getting in the car with him!

"You can't take this car," he said. "You can take the other one, but I can't let you go in *this*."

I almost didn't trust him, but then he started getting the girls out of the backseat and grabbing all of his personal belongings.

"Did he have a tracker or something on that car?" I thought.

I couldn't worry about that detail. The car I was in had a 95-percent chance of dying on the highway.

So, I waited and watched to make sure he had too many things in his hand to worry about me — or, at least enough to slow him down. Then, I made my move; dashing for the driver's side door.

He just stood there and watched.

Eventually, we pulled out of the parking lot in separate cars. We were finally headed in opposite directions.

Chapter 17: Things People Don't Tell You When You Leave

You'll look over your shoulder and stare deeply into your rear-view mirror.

You'll take side streets instead of the Interstate.

God forbid that he sees you.

There's no telling what he'd do.

You'll get asked about the lavish diamond on your finger.

The leasing agent, dreaming of her own big day, won't realize you're already sporting a wedding band — yet you've requested a one-bedroom apartment.

Like you said, "It's just you."

You'll take unannounced days off, at a time when your boss most needs you.

What good would you be with swollen eyes from all the tears you've cried and days-old clothes?

You might not even have a toothbrush.

The crying fits will go on repeatedly.

The tears aren't for him, though, or the love you thought you had.

You're daydreaming (or is it a nightmare?) about the moment you'll have to tell coworkers, friends, and family what *really* happened.

Maybe you'll never do that.

Maybe they'll never know.

You told him you wouldn't stay, and he did it again.

His hands to your body.

You had to go.

You'll smile while having jam sessions in your car. You'll listen to whatever makes you feel free.

Music is what gets you through the laundry list of things you need to do:

Move your clothes.

Grab your documents.

Find an apartment.

Change banking accounts.

Change passwords.

Google "file for a divorce".

You'll question yourself.

Maybe it's when you're packing up your purses or shoes, TV or your computer?

A voice will whisper, *"You Can't Do This!"*

You'll have to respond with fervency or else the uncertainty will consume you.

"I'm going to be okay."

"I'm going to be okay."

"I'm going to be okay."

Shaking, you'll say these words.

Afraid, you'll say these words — but nothing else.

There'll be no room for doubt.

Except doubt keeps knocking.

Like, when you put the deposit down on your new apartment.

What's $99 when you love the place?

Plus, it's got a security gate to keep him out and a swanky feel!

For some reason though, you'll find yourself pacing back and forth in front of the leasing office.

That voice will whisper again, "*Are you sure you guys can't work it out?*"

You'll need to be reminded daily, by the ones who love you most, why you left and why you can't go back.

"This will only build," your Dad will say.

A friend will remind you, "They never start out with a punch."

When no one is available to talk, you'll have to close your eyes and recall the fear you felt, the rage in his eyes, and the way your heartbeat pulsed deep within your chest.

Remember when you tried to get to the door and he blocked your exit?

He had your keys and phone, remember?

He was standing in front of the door, remember?

When those pictures are too painful to see, you'll have to force yourself to hear.

The change in his tone right before he leaped across the couch toward you.

Or the whisper of your friends' voice the night you left.

"*You have to get out of that situation,*" she said softly. "*You hear me?*"

She didn't want her husband to overhear.

You'll have to force yourself to remember how affirming her words were in your panicked state because now, you're calm. Now, you're free.

Now, you're "safe".

And should you forget any of this, his "I'm sorry" and "I miss you" texts may become too powerful to ignore.

Remember this: if he hit you, pushed you, or beat you down with his words — ***You. Deserve. Better.***

You'll lean on friends for a listening ear, but you'll quickly learn even the best of them can't truly grasp the pain behind your endless rants.

You'll talk in circles; detailing past arguments and putting a voice to the questions you can't answer.

"I don't understand why he wouldn't just get a divorce?" you'll ask.

"Why was he so angry with me? What did I do?"

Yet, amid deep thought, you'll make cliché statements that sound like you've got it all figured out.

"I don't know girl, I just want to be happy."

Or…

"I'm not sad, I'm just a little *surprised*."

Right.

Although life will seem like it's crashing down on you, you'll also learn just how strong you truly are.

You'll ignore the voice that tells you to quit your job and move back home.

You'll silence the lie that you can't focus enough to go to work.

You'll punch the clock with your head held high.

When coworkers inquire about your absence with questions like *"Is everything okay?"*

You'll simply respond "*Yes*," with a poker face because you'll have learned by now, that you don't owe anyone an explanation.

From this point forward, you're going with your gut; the gut that told you moving home would stunt your growth.

This moment in time is for your development.

You're moving from caterpillar to butterfly.

From chicken to eagle.

Running won't do you any good.

It's that very voice that you've ignored for so long.

The one that told you, you weren't okay, you weren't safe and you weren't loved — at least not by him.

It's alright, though.

You're listening now.

If you're anything like me, you'll realize that all those times you thought God would be angry with you for leaving, were a lie.

You'll find favor you didn't expect.

Deals. Discounts. His mercy. His embrace.

And last but not least, grace for the foolishness your soon-to-be-ex may send via email or text.

Trust me. It'll come.

He's grieving too.

The day will arrive when you sign the papers and dissolve your marriage.

You'll swear with your right hand that the information presented is true.

"Have one or more of you lived in the state for the past six months?"

"Do you have any children?"

"Is the wife pregnant?"

"Yes."

"No."

"No."

Thank God.

The moment will be nostalgic.

Tears will fall as you realize just a little more than a year before, you stood in the exact courthouse with your right hands raised; seconds from obtaining your marriage license.

Who would've known it would end this way?

You'll wonder why you're crying.

Meanwhile, he'll show no emotion.

Your nose will run.

There will never seem to be enough space on the wad of tissue you grabbed from the restroom.

He'll try to start up a conversation.

Then, a second or third tissue run will become the perfect escape.

He'll try to pry for information.

"Do you have your keys with you?" he'll ask.

A chill will run down your spine.

It's an attempt to see if you have a new keychain linking you to a new complex or your new car. He'll so desperately want to know the model and make.

Your fear will transition to anger. You'll want to punch him in the face as he continues asking questions.

"Are you sure this is what you want?" he'll say.

He'll make counterfeit claims based on a love he never had for you.

"It breaks my heart to see you like this!"

"How?" you'll wonder. "You broke me!"

As your fury swirls, you'll choose to hold your composure.

Deputies are just feet away.

Armed deputies.

You'd best act civil.

You'll wait for what seems like hours for the clerk to give you formal instructions.

You'll learn that in just 20 days, you'll return from Mrs. to Miss; pending, of course, the judge's decision.

Eventually, the two of you will walk out.

You'll stare at his back as he struggles to figure out if he should slow his pace.

You'll ponder speeding up.

Are there any final words? No.

As the doors close, you'll split in different directions and then, turn for one last glimpse.

He's got his hands on his hips walking slowly as if he's just finished a morning run. Really, he's just in deep thought.

It's déjà vu round two.

You'll remember holding those hands the day you got the marriage license, and how the two of you walked around this same path.

You'll remember how bright your future looked then and how dismal it looks now.

From there, you'll go into hiding.

After all, why the hell did he have so many questions?

Hiding your new address.

Hiding your new phone number.

Oh, speaking of that.

If he opened your phone account, getting a new one will be top priority.

Trust me, he'll remind you of the pending closure.

Just when you think you've reached a calm, you'll find out details that'll piss you off.

"Would you like to upgrade to unlimited data?" the phone store rep will ask.

"It looks like he only set your phone up with three gigabytes."

No wonder your internet was always running slow each month!

What a jerk.

Debts may arise that you didn't expect.

If it stems from some dumb decision you made together, arguing will be pointless.

You'll learn that once he's been to the courthouse, he's done being cordial.

It's too real at that point.

There's paperwork filed, and money spent to file it.

You'll no longer make phone calls to your husband at work.

He'll no longer bring in the lunches you packed each night.

There'll be no pictures of him or her on your Instagram or Facebook for weeks.

Family will come to check on you, you'll post in excitement, but your spouse will be nowhere in sight.

People will begin to ask questions.

While your new place will be filled with things — like inspirational wall art and flowers you picked out for yourself — loneliness will linger in the air.

You'll go to therapy if you're smart.

There's no sense in failing to recover and repeating the same mistakes.

You'll be forced to open up about all the embarrassing details you thought you'd hide.

How you stayed despite him putting his hands on you.

How you somehow failed to realize his epic rants on your personality, character, and appearance weren't just day-to-day disagreements.

You'll fight tears because you want to appear strong to offset the weakness your story portrays.

Your therapist will ask questions that puncture your ego.

Only then, will you realize, you had some nerve walking in with one.

In your eyes, you did nothing wrong.

You'll say, *"I wasn't the abuser. I didn't beat on anyone."*

"I tried everything to make it work."

"I was loyal."

"I didn't tell a soul."

"I prayed for him."

"I used my faith."

"Do you think there are any signs you missed?" your therapist will ask, "because we, as women, often confuse control and manipulation for love."

You'll stare blankly in her direction.

You'll know her statement isn't a suggestion but a factual analysis of your short time together.

Your first response will be, "*No*".

But eventually, if you want to gain anything from the experience, you'll circle around to talk about the red flags you made disappear.

She'll tell you you're numb.

She'll warn you, "*you're going to feel it.*"

Perhaps once it's finalized?

Maybe, the day of the hearing?

Her diagnosis will confirm your fears, that maybe you *do* need someone to come with you to the courthouse again?

Maybe you really *do* need to take some time off that week?

Should you resist the urge to stay at home on Sundays, people at church will put two and two together.

"She's here, but where's he?" they'll wonder.

"Call me some time, we can talk," they'll offer.

"If you ever want to hang out, let me know," another will say.

Hugs will last longer, accompanied by additional back rubs and shoulder squeezes.

You'll smile because, at this point, you haven't quite figured out what to say.

Smiling is difficult when you're angry, though.

When your bank account starts getting low, you'll get pissed because he's the reason you had to spend your part of the money on an all-new life.

You'll be furious you agreed to split what was in the accounts.

"*I should've taken it all,*" you'll say.

You'll regret the day you met him.

For certain, the day you put that ring on.

What a freaking monster!

Who pretends they want to be with someone and then changes their mind hours after they've made their vows?

You'll yell when you can't figure out a way to purchase what you need, or the weight of handling your own finances becomes too heavy.

If you're not careful, your downward spiral will just keep spinning.

You'll sob on your bed while writing awful things about him in your journal no one will ever need to read.

You'll cry yourself to sleep.

The weeping will endure for a night, but I assure you, every time, joy will come in the morning.

Scripture.

It will all come back to you if it was there before.

When you rise each day, that still, small voice inside of you will recall all the ordinary things that were actually blessings from above.

The protection provided.

The exit ramps your eyes were opened to see.

That voice will remind you that you're no longer there. You're no longer being hurt or talked down to. No longer walking on eggshells. No more constantly "missing the mark."

You'll realize that's enough to be thankful for, in itself.

You'll be reminded to count it all joy and challenged to throw a party for this trial you're in.

It will sound preposterous.

"A party?" you'll think.

Your bruised heart won't feel like dancing.

This will be the ultimate test.

To start over. To be single again. To choose the "divorcee" box on an application.

To go to court, stand before a judge and answer the questions that make your troubled marriage seem so simple.

"Is the marriage irrevocably broken?" the judge will ask.

"Yes," you'll say in unison.

And…that'll be it.

"But he pushed me to the ground!"

"But he stuffed socks in my face!"

"But he wrestled me in the kitchen!"

"But he dragged me across the carpet in our bedroom!"

"My neck hurt for days!"

All those thoughts won't matter.

He won't pay for them — at least not in the legal system.

Yet, you'll be reminded that this chapter is now over.

Times when family and friends cringed at his harsh words.

Times where he assured you, you'd never amount to anything.

You'll remember how it felt to try and quickly downplay your goals, especially in front of his friends.

Times when your head hung low.

Times when you cried yourself to sleep.

Times when you pulled him to the side to hide another tirade.

Times when you felt defeated because your beauty and charm were just never enough.

Even if it seems distant, you'll know from this point on, things will get better.

Chapter 18: Sir Talk-A-Lot

He just wouldn't shut up.

That's all I can remember about the day we got divorced. My Ex was being "Chatty Kathy" in that courtroom.

I walked in just in time for our case to be heard. I decided I wasn't taking off work for this crap, so I had to rush over after the morning show. It was a group setting. Apparently, dozens of other couples had decided to call it quits, too.

"*So, how have you been?*" he asked.

I rolled my eyes.

My skin crawled hearing the sound of his voice.

We didn't *have* to sit together. In fact, I had every mind to head straight for the other side of the room. The only problem was, he halfway jumped up out of his seat when I walked in; waving like an idiot as if I couldn't find his shitty face in the crowd.

Surprisingly? It was over in like 30 minutes. The whole ordeal wasn't so bad — besides him running his mouth and asking about my family. Oh, and answering the judge's questions for me!

"Does the wife want to return to her maiden name?" the judge asked.

"YES!" My Ex screamed into the mic.

I should've slapped him upside the head and made him eat that metal on the microphone. He had to be kidding!

"You think I want YOUR last name?" I thought.

I was livid.

Good thing it was over.

OIL POUR

Watching my Ex run his mouth in court that day reminds me of how much he loved words, as long as they were about him. *Words of affirmation,* he assured me, were his love language. To survive the relationship, I wrote countless notes, cards, and letters scribbled on lined paper ripped from my journal. I was putting my journalism degree to work. Some of those notes were damn near poetry.

"Happy Birthday, baby! On your day, I want you to know ALL that I feel. You're like 1 in a million! There's literally no one like you! I'm talking inside and out! Your eyes are soft and bright, but deep-set, *brimming with meaning, like wells of water.*"

Ugh.

If you ever had the opportunity to read through all of the cards and notes I wrote him (FYI: You won't), you'd find the same, pathetic language, as well as an abundance of scripture references. The one italicized above is Song of Solomon 5:12. Do you know how freaking desperate you have to be to go find a verse in Song of Solomon? That book isn't even in any of the Bibles I own!

I digress.

There were several issues here. One, I didn't feel the things I wrote. Two, the scriptures were mandatory. He demanded them and would give me an earful if his precious letters weren't biblically-based. In yet another "teaching moment", he explained that this was the way he wanted to be addressed:

Praise him.

Flatter him.

Insert Bible verse.

Pray for him.

Love, Jazmin.

So, I followed the formula and I wrote lies. I forced myself to focus on the one, rare day he did something kind and exaggerated my feelings to fill the pages.

My embellished stories spilled over onto social media as well. I called him the *love of my life* on Instagram and Facebook, alongside pictures of those roses I mentioned earlier in the book. I told my followers he bought them "just because". Yeah, right. He bought those flowers because he lost it during an argument and decided to twist my arms until my skin itched and burned. Hours later, the roses and a card were on the kitchen table. Just because? No, just no.

Let this be a warning: Don't buy into your friends' excessive, romantic social media posts — especially if you start to see less and less of them in person. If they've gone ghost, call them. If they're defensive when you approach, give them a hug and tell them you love them. If they seem to pull back even further, keep sending texts. Don't pry. Just make them smile. Make them laugh. Keep in contact. This is exactly what abusers don't want you to do. Don't let your friend believe the lie that she's alone. Even if she doesn't respond or give you the same love in return, love on her anyway! The one friend who constantly tried to call me, text me, or hang out during my marriage is the *first person* I called for help when I left.

Thank God for her.

Think of all your friendships. Have any changed as the result of a new love interest? Remind yourself of how it felt to lose more and more of that friend. After reading my story, how would you handle a similar situation differently?

____

____

____

____

____

____

____

____

Chapter 19: Dodging Pain

As a newly-divorced person, you have to have discernment when taking others' advice. You have to realize that the people in your life don't want you to experience any additional pain. They will literally do anything to make sure you don't have another sleepless night. However, pain makes you change. Pain helps you grow.

Ask yourself: Do I want to grow? Or do I want to stay in the same place my tragedy left me?

Shortly after my divorce, those closest to me suggested I needed a friend; a male friend. They encouraged me to call my ex-boyfriend from college.

"Maybe you could just talk?" they said. "You know…and have someone listen."

The same thought had crossed my mind a couple of times, but I had so much shame and guilt associated with the way that relationship ended. I didn't know how I would be received. I also didn't know what either of us would gain by opening that door again.

Months later, and despite my better judgment, I ignored those two unknowns and began to engage in daily conversations with this person. It felt safe talking with him. He was understanding and compassionate. He supported me and most of all, he renewed my faith that all men weren't crazy.

At the same time, my therapist was telling me to stay away from relationships for a year. A whole year! It seemed like an eternity, and that's not surprising, considering my situation.

For example, I had taken off my wedding ring, but I was still cooking up a storm. I was preparing meals as if two people needed breakfast, lunch, and dinner. My reality said single, but my mind was stuck on taken. So naturally, I was searching for someone to fill the void.

"Take this time for yourself," my therapist warned me. "Figure out what you want."

As she spoke, I remember sitting in her wingback chair, digging my nails into the cherry brown leather. I felt like I was Chris in *Get Out.* Please tell me you've seen that epic horror movie?

For those of you who haven't, Chris is the main character. In one scene, he evades hypnosis by picking cotton fibers from a chair's armrest. Eventually, he uses the cotton to plug his ears and ignore the doctor's words.

Like Chris, I didn't want to hear anything my therapist had to say. I didn't want to be brainwashed into believing I was broken. No, I wanted to believe I was healed and that I could quickly hop into another relationship and never look back. I rejected the idea that the abuse had changed me for the worse.

As hard as I tried, I couldn't drown out my therapist's voice. I heard her loud and clear and I knew her advice was solid, but I had questions! I had already started talking to my ex-boyfriend again. Now what? Break it off? Things were just getting good!

She warned me to not give any men direct access.

"Don't give out your phone number," she said. "Send emails. Use Facebook messenger."

She told me I would feel overwhelmed if I went too quickly. Little did she know, my ex-boyfriend text me before my appointment and I was startled. I felt stressed trying to figure out what to say and how to respond. I jumped every time my ringer alerted me to a new message.

Sitting there, alone in my car, I felt even more inadequate. Why couldn't I be a normal 27-year-old? Why did I lack the confidence to talk to someone of the opposite sex?

She was right. It was too much, too soon.

My focus should have been on all of my internal pain. Instead, I fell into a romantic daze. My ex-boyfriend and I were picking up right where we left off —planning Caribbean escapes and holiday visits. If I'm honest, we were planning to spend the rest of our lives together, but neither of us wanted to say it!

While it seemed harmless, it was so dangerous. He was ready for love. He wanted to settle down. Meanwhile, a part of me was screaming to be free — from all my suffering and the limitations of my previous relationship. I was no longer married but still felt trapped by all of my Ex's words and actions. He criticized every part of me, down to the way I loved and showed support. I wondered if I could ever do another person any good? Did I really have it in me to be a great wife? I tried so hard and seemingly failed. I didn't want to feel that pain again.

I also had this romanticized idea of getting back into the dating scene. Before settling down again, I imagined myself testing the waters to "see what was out there". No commitments. No titles. Just good old plain fun.

"Yeah, I don't see myself getting married for like…another three to five years or something," I confessed one night on the phone.

My ex-boyfriend was shocked, but deep down, I think he believed I would change my mind.

"You're just hurt," he reasoned. "You just need time."

There's something people need to realize about divorcees: They can be selfish, really selfish.

I'll speak for myself and say, I was so used to compromising with my spouse, that I had a chip on my shoulder. In my mind, I was robbed of my time, effort, and energy. I felt the entire world needed to pay me back. I had my loving moments but for the most part, I didn't care about other people, their feelings, or their problems. If it wasn't about me, I was sort of numb.

Divorcees will stomp on your heart in a second. Some, like myself, won't even realize they're doing it. Others will do it intentionally.

Did I mention my Ex (husband) was recently-separated from his first wife when I met him? He never told me what caused her to move out. I have my guesses, but I suppose I'll never know the truth.

Back then, other than reminding myself not to mess around with a married man, I didn't think much of his relationship status. I really didn't understand the depths of his pain and I naively compared his annulment to a bad high school breakup. After all, they were only married for a couple of weeks!

It was a delicate situation. He seemed normal, so I never wanted to pry.

Anything we went through in our dating phase, I chalked up to ignorant male behavior.

Was he hard to read? Committed one day and distant the next?

"Yeah, but aren't all men like that at some point?" I thought.

Unfortunately, it wasn't that clear-cut.

If someone says they've been married before, you need to investigate. In fact, you should investigate everyone, but definitely a divorcee!

If they try to convince you that "it just didn't work out" or "we just didn't get along," keep asking questions! You don't have to be insensitive, but if the person you're dating is talking about starting a life with you, you deserve to know the details. I'd even advise you to look up their records. Be certain you're not dealing with a habitual abuser or cheater who's simply looking to prey on another loving soul.

I also encourage you to ask if they've gone to counseling. Just remember: they may be offended, or at least, defensive. Therapy is a touchy subject for some, but it's still necessary! If this person hasn't gone to see a counselor and insists they'll never go, you should let them go. All of those emotions tied to their feelings of abandonment, failure, and distrust are bound to surface at some point. Do you want them to take it out on you? Do you want them to drag you through their emotional hell? Is anyone really worth all that? I suppose my ex-boyfriend was willing to find out.

I went to Jamaica with him. Who goes to *Jamaica* with a guy they're not dating? Please. We talked every day, met up several times in a year, read The Wait together and he was the only person I wanted to call with my good news. That was my man. We just didn't have titles. I wasn't claiming him.

That's something I'll never be proud of. I became the guy I always despised.

When we arrived on our vacation, he had so many surprises planned. He thought of me ahead of time. He listened to things I wanted to do. This wasn't new. This was the excellence he always presented in a relationship. He cared about the details.

I was thrilled to hear him say he'd already planned for us to go horseback riding. It had been on my bucket list for years! At the same time, the gesture made me feel so…unworthy.

I hadn't considered him at all. What did he want out of this trip? One thing's for sure, he deserved so much better. I cry every time I think of how I wasn't emotionally there for him. I know that won't ever make up for what I did and even though I've asked for forgiveness, it still hurts.

The pain I felt only amplified the day I called and told him we should stop talking. I had to make the call, though. I saw the path we were heading down. A rocky relationship and marriage would've been the only logical next steps for us. Later on, I would've resented him just as my ex-husband resented me. My Ex wasn't healed when we met, and I wasn't healed, now. I was the only one who could break the cycle.

When divorcees, or anyone who just got out of a long-term relationship, realize that the time they spend alone after a breakup isn't just for them (or their therapist's ego), it's so much easier to commit to growth!

You can't just be out here recklessly damaging people.

Hurt people really do hurt other people and I cared about my ex-boyfriend too much to continue to let him down. I also knew my personal healing couldn't take place if we existed in any form of relationship. I would have forced my pain onto him. I definitely wouldn't have continued counseling. Who knows if I would've been any better off? He surely wouldn't have.

As soon as you realize, that you, in your current state, are neither ready for or deserving of another person's presence, it's time to release them. That's love in action; stopping yourself from damaging another person, no matter how bad it hurts.

Is this a novel idea? No, but so many dismiss the advice. People — friends and family — make it easy to ignore! I did.

After my divorce, my friends encouraged me to get on Bumble, the dating app.

They also set up nights for us to hit the town and get as many numbers as we could. Sounds harmless, right?

Well, I'd get all dressed up — in something that was still reasonably modest because all I owned were the clothes my Ex wanted me to wear — and then, I'd be lost. My friends seemed to be having fun, talking with guys at the bar or lounge, but when a guy turned to me, I'd lose my ability to speak.

"What are you — a mute?" one guy asked at a party.

I froze, and my eyes started to water. He didn't mean any harm. His question was relevant. I gulped and silently coached myself through the meltdown.

"You will NOT cry in the middle of this dance floor!" I thought. "Absolutely not!"

The party was an adult game night. Imagine hundreds of 20 and 30-something's on multiple floors doing the electric slide, playing Twister, and even musical chairs.

My friends wanted me to volunteer for the last game, but for some reason, I was apprehensive.

This wasn't our first time at the event, but I couldn't remember why I felt so uneasy about a few rounds of musical chairs.

"I need a couple more pretty ladies on the dance floor!" the host called out.

"Jaz! Just go!" my friends said.

Let me reiterate this fact: your friends and family care and their hearts are really in the right place when they offer alternative ways for you to deal with your pain. However, despite anything I said about wanting a man, all I really needed was a night out with *them*. I wasn't ready for a *him*.

The musical chairs game got raunchy, quickly.

Immediately, it all clicked. I knew where this was heading, and I didn't want to be a part. Men were sitting in each chair. So, when the music stopped, you had to drop yourself on top of one of them. That wasn't the problem. That was the easy part. By the second or third round, chairs were being taken away and the host had to up the ante.

"Alright, y'all. When the music stops," he said. "We need you to find a chair and give that man a nice little dance."

My palms started sweating. I watched as the host pulled another chair from beside my right leg. I looked down and then out at the crowd.

For the past two years, the only interaction I'd had with a man was so traumatizing.

I could hear the voice of my Ex ringing in my ears.

"What are you doing?"

"God! Why are you so awkward?!"

"Seriously? Just move!"

His words made me so uncomfortable in my own skin. I feared looking into another man's eyes, even for a second, and giving him the opportunity to hurt me. I couldn't go there. I just couldn't.

The host must have sensed my apprehension. I was still in a daze when he grabbed my arm and gently pulled me aside.

"I'm sorry, sweetie," he said. "You cute…but you gotta go."

That was the second strike; another gut-wrenching wound to my self-esteem that was already shattered. I wanted to fade away.

"Cute, but not good enough?" I thought. "Story of my life!"

You cannot dodge pain. It's going to come no matter what.

In my experience, trying to avoid the agony of being single — loving on myself, going places alone, or making major life decisions without someone to affirm me — only deepened my wounds.

Chapter 20: Depression Is Real

Six months after my divorce, I was severely depressed. I didn't know until I returned home from my 28th birthday trip to London.

I suppose all the planning — booking train tickets, flights to Amsterdam, tea at the museum, and a night at the theater — kept my mind off what I was really feeling.

I came back to the States with a cold and I wasn't surprised. There were so many people in Europe who coughed into the plane aisles! No wonder I got sick.

The cough and sore throat didn't go away for months. I kept taking off work to fight it and found myself spending more and more time, alone, in my apartment. I *felt* lonely. The adrenaline rush that traveling provides had run out.

This was the beginning of my sunken state; the place where I couldn't be happy about anything. Suddenly, I hated my job, I hated Florida and I didn't want to be involved at my church.

I also didn't want to hang out with the friends I'd made, and I was secretly making my exit plan.

The months passed by quickly. I focused my attention on not enjoying the life I had, and instead, spoke into existence that I wasn't going to be in Florida much longer. I'm a firm believer in creating the life you want to see, with your words.

For some reason, I felt God *owed me* a fresh start. There just seemed to be so much pain in Orlando. I didn't want to face it anymore.

After I separated from my Ex, I stayed. He left. He quit. He moved. I kept my job. I made myself believe I was strong.

In the immediate aftermath of the divorce, I only took off one day to grieve. *One day.* That's honestly all I thought I needed to process the hell I'd been through.

That was silly.

I stopped going to therapy because I reasoned myself out of it. My counselor suggested that I make a dream board with her, and that's when I lost it.

“I'm not about to pay her $45 to make a dream board,” I thought. “I can do that at home…by myself.”

The ex-boyfriend I was talking to would listen to most of my foolishness and see right through me. I hated that, too.

He knew I was tired; emotionally, physically, and mentally from all that had happened. He knew I was just being reckless.

Each day, with both my actions and my words, I let a little piece of what I worked so hard to obtain, slip through my grasp.

On Saturdays, I sat assessing how much money I'd need to move to Washington, D.C. It was a dream of mine to live there. Why? Well, for two years after college, Virginia was my home and I fell in love! Washington D.C. was the last place I remembered feeling *happy.*

Maybe that's why, in addition to the UK, Jamaica, Philly (to see Beyoncé in the rain), and Michigan — I flew to D.C. like four times in a matter of months. I was always on a flight because, in Orlando, I felt trapped.

My estimations told me the move was going to be costly. I wouldn't have a job, at least, not at first. I would still have to pay for my car and student loans. With all those factors combined, I didn't see how I was going to do it, but I was determined.

I didn't want anyone telling me how to live my life. I didn't want to feel weighed down by the pressure of doing what was expected. I wanted to make my own rules.

Really, I wanted to quit.

I believe that’s one of the dangers of divorce. Breaking a marital bond makes retreating from anything else seem so easy, especially in my case. In Florida, a simple dissolution of marriage only took 20 days!

Not even a month, and my Ex disappeared! I wanted to feel that same, euphoric sense of freedom in every area of my life, but that's just it. It's just a feeling! He was gone, but I still had issues!

Once you have a major "failure" in life, like a divorce, you have to be careful not to approach everything — your career, family life, friendships, even your dreams — from that perspective. Life isn't always *simple*. If you're not careful, you'll glorify your failures and the idea of a quick fix.

Trust me, even if you quit your job, move or start cutting ties with old friends, you're still going to have to address your problems. If you're unwilling to do so and continue to back out of every single commitment, you'll never get anywhere.

This was a pivotal moment in my story. I needed to fight. I needed to resist the urge to give up. I needed help…but I was too proud to ask anyone for it.

Thankfully, I ended up moving in with the very friends I was trying to reject. They became counselors-of-sorts through my various dramatic episodes. Moving in with them meant I was no longer alone. If I cried? Well, someone was going to hear, see or check. They weren't going to let me stay in bed for an entire day. I was grateful for that.

I was also grateful I wouldn't have to sign a real lease. I was still planning to leave and didn't want to make any more commitments to Florida. I assured the girls I'd be out of their hair shortly.

Doesn't that sound familiar?

Writing this makes me realize even more, how abusers force their behavior off on their victims. Like my Ex, during that brief period where we bounced from house-to-house, I was now dodging commitment at the expense of my health and peace.

While I really enjoyed talks with the girls and even making dinner together, I knew I likely wouldn't be able to sleep with their work schedules.

In those days, I could not focus. Anything could get my attention. Someone making food at 11pm? The sound of a TV down the hall? It was too much stimulation for me to handle. My mind was already spinning.

"I wanna go to Greece."

"Did I pay that bill?"

"Crap, I forgot to call my mom."

"Ooooh!! This dress is cute!"

"Ugh! My back. It hurts."

"Nobody likes me here."

"You know what? I'm done eating meat."

"Wow! Hugh Hefner died?"

"I suck."

I'd have entire conversations, just like this one (with myself, by the way), in less than a minute. I just couldn't shut my mind off and I would do anything to not rest! At some point, my strained sleep schedule caught up with me and I started having a re-occurring thought.

"I don't want to get out of bed."

This wasn't a normal drowsy state, though. I couldn't just push through it. *If* I woke up to the sound of my alarm, I would just lay there in extreme sadness. I couldn't get up. I felt bound.

So, I started sleeping in. I'd press snooze once, twice or even three times to avoid my wake-up call. Other nights, I would wait so late to wear myself out, that I'd forget to set an alarm altogether. Until one day, I missed an entire morning show. Then, it happened again….and again.

In the eight years I'd worked in morning TV, I had never *missed* a show. Time off? Sure. Scheduled absence? Sure. Running late this morning? Of course. But completely missing it? Like arriving at work and the 5AM morning newscast is over? This was new territory, and it was starting to scare the crap out of me!

I had anxiety for months about waking up late. It was just one more item on the list of things keeping my mind on fast-forward.

On mornings where I slept through the beeping, my roommates would wake up to the sound of me spilling combs, brushes, and hairpins out of plastic containers and onto the floor. I was moving too fast; dropping every tool I needed as my hands shook in fear.

This was around the time I started wearing my natural curls on TV.

I hadn't mastered the style yet and I felt this immense pressure to be perfect. I couldn't let Black women down. People would talk about me if my curls weren't immaculately coiled. My hair was already *different.* I couldn't just rush out of the house.

My roommate would watch as I repeatedly turned the water in the shower on and off again. I couldn't think. My mind blocked me from making a decision. I couldn't figure out if I had enough time to wet my hair.

"Can I help you with anything?" she'd ask.

"No," I'd cry.

Streams of tears would run down my face as I brushed my teeth, mixing in perfectly with the foam surrounding my lips.

I stared in the mirror and was both terrified and humiliated by the idea of walking in late to work again. I knew what it looked like. I knew what they were thinking. "*She must really not care.*"

The truth is, I wanted to be present. I didn't understand why I couldn't connect with any of the stories we were sharing. On camera, I looked like a ghost! I was so distant from my work and all the people in the newsroom.

Slowly and silently, I was being robbed of my value. I started to believe I didn't belong in the position I had been given. I didn't think I was deserving anymore.

It was time for me to get a new alarm and wake the hell up — on so many levels. I was well on my way to having nothing.

Then, I heard something; something I desperately needed to know.

Chapter 21: Slaying Giants

A little more than a year after my divorce, I was invited to speak at a woman's empowerment event and I'm convinced it was a destiny moment. God wanted me there, if for nothing else, then to *finally* get my attention.

The host wanted me to speak about my marriage and the abuse. A month prior, she watched a video on my Facebook page where I briefly discussed some of the details. I wanted to do my part for Domestic Violence Awareness Month, but I never thought someone would invite me to speak on the topic.

Sitting up on stage that night, something miraculous happened. I answered each question to the best of my ability and was vulnerable in ways I never planned, but then, my *ears* opened.

"*Oh my God!*" one woman whispered to a friend. "*I knew it! That's the girl from the news!*"

Her friend leaned over to get a better look. "*Oh, wow. You're right. I love her! I watch her every day!*"

I tried to keep my focus by talking louder into the mic, but I couldn't drown out their voices. All over the room, I could hear women expressing their love for me and giving me compliments. It was so odd.

"How am I hearing this?" I thought.

"*Wow!*" another woman said while clutching her chest. Something I mentioned about my Ex left her in shock. "*I remember when they got married!*"

The event host didn't use my photo or name on the flyer. I wasn't expecting her to, but I suppose that's why everyone in the audience was so surprised to see me and hear my story.

Once I passed the mic to the next speaker, I sat there trying to comprehend what was happening. I grabbed my own chest. Something was going on in *my* heart. I could feel it.

"These people love me?" I thought. "I'm not even an anchor on the main channel. They watch me every day?"

For months, I had wrestled with the idea of throwing in the towel: on news, on God and on Florida. Now, I wondered, if, after all the turmoil, embarrassment, and loss, God knew that all I needed was to feel supported? That maybe if someone just hugged me, held me, and told me they cared, I'd put my fists down and stop fighting the inevitable?

I think that's exactly what happened. On stage, I could feel the words brewing in the depths of my soul.

"I don't want to leave here!" I thought. "Why would I leave? There's so much happening here!"

I should clarify: this wasn't about fame or notoriety. I looked out in the crowd and saw women with life coach businesses, limousine services, hair salons, and franchises. There were prophetesses in the crowd, sitting next to therapists, accountants, authors, and app developers. I was amazed because this thriving community of successful women existed — and they welcomed *me*. The whole part about them recognizing my face from the news? That was just icing on the cake.

If I'm honest, I wasn't just chasing a new job in a new city. I was looking for the thing I was always *meant* to do. I wanted to know why I was here on this Earth.

I felt like the marriage had stolen so much of my time that I'd never be able to get back. I didn't want to waste another year. I knew there had to be something more.

In seconds, God opened my eyes and ears to see what friends, family, and pastors had been trying to say for months. I had something special in Orlando; something many don't ever get a chance to experience. I had a community and whether they knew it or not, that night was the first step into my purpose.

Women, young and old, walked up to me to share how much my story inspired them or gave them hope for a friend in a similar situation. That blessed my heart!

"What took me so long?" I thought.

I had to remind myself that all that time I spent ignoring God's signs didn't matter. I understood *now*. It was time for me to plant roots and stop allowing what happened in my past to derail my future.

I did have a call. I did have a purpose. It was time to go after it. I had a book to write. I had stories to tell. I had a testimony to share.

It's funny; that event was called "Giant Slayers" and I had a Goliath-sized challenge coming my way. Before I could really be effective, I had to conquer it; once and for all. That giant was *within*.

Chapter 22: Nothing But A Liar

I think I was driving home from work the first time it hit me.

"*He lied,*" I thought.

It had been nearly two years since my Ex went to jail due to our altercation. Hours before that incident, I bought the most amazing bottle of perfume. I am not ashamed to say, I still have that empty container of Anna Sui's *La Nuit de Boheme.* The gold butterfly topper is just too fabulous to throw out, even if the contents are gone.

Purchasing that perfume at *Ross Dress For Les*s was risky. I couldn't test what was inside the $11 box unless I committed to buying it. So, I swiped my bank card and headed straight for the car.

Something about this fragrance smelled *wild.* It gave me a rush of energy. It was warm; like passion and bonfire embers. Yet, the floral notes made me feel delicate and feminine. That night, when my Ex walked in the door, I stuck my whole wrist in his face.

"SMELL!" I demanded with a huge grin.

"Ugh! What is that?" He asked while swiping my arm away.

I was so caught up in the scent, I didn't even notice his criticism. I could breathe in that perfume all day!

"You don't like it!?" I asked with my nose buried in my forearm.

"Jaz, don't ever wear that again — EVER," he said.

He then proceeded to tell me that I didn't know how to choose a perfume. He also promised he would take me to a luxury department store and *teach me* at a later date.

First of all, he and I both knew no such trip to a luxury department store was ever going to happen. He wasn't spending any money on me unless he had to. Secondly, my choice was just fine. Where the hell did he get off telling me what I "knew how" to do?

This was such a classic abuser move. He twisted my reality to convince me that something I knew was true — wasn't. That perfume was to die for! He just wouldn't admit it. He didn't want me out in the world making sound decisions and using my own brain. No! He wanted me to question myself and doubt my own judgment. Sadly, it worked.

On a few other occasions, I secretly sprayed the perfume, but he kept scolding me! Eventually, I got tired of hearing his mouth. I threw the bottle into an old purse and vowed to never wear it again. I knew I'd struck gold with that perfume, but after a while, his consistent disapproval changed my mind.

I thought, "Maybe it really does smell awful?"

Months after the divorce, while trying to find a dress for work, the embellished bottle fell onto the floor of my closet.

"Oh my God!" I squealed while bending down to pick it up.

It was a real 'Eureka, I found it!' moment and it didn't end there. I doused myself in that perfume; letting the mist hit all the major pulse points — my wrists, neck, inner elbow, and behind my ear. The fragrance was just as invigorating as the day I bought it.

I walked into work that morning with confidence. I was so happy! I found my perfume! I hadn't even thought about someone else smelling it. I loved it. That's all that mattered.

"What is that you're wearing?"

Upon hearing this question, I froze. My co-anchor, who had obviously picked up on the scent, was waiting for me to answer. I just couldn't tell if he liked what he smelled or if his nostrils were on fire. My worst fear was that my Ex was *actually* right. My palms started sweating.

"Ummm…I can't pronounce the name," I said quickly. I hoped he'd just move on.

"Oh. I just asked because it smells amazing," he said. "I would buy some of that for my wife!"

I smiled the whole workday and all the way home.

"Yeah, my Ex totally lied!"

Isn't it crazy, how we're wired to believe anything we consistently hear? That's why affirmations and positive self-talk are so important. If you say it long enough, you can convince your mind to accept it as truth.

Unfortunately, my Ex said so many negative things to me, that even two years after the divorce, his voice was drowning out my own.

"I hate my skin."

"Omg! I look a mess!"

"Look at these dark circles under my eyes."

"Ugh. I need to gain some weight."

"Yikes!"

Those are just some of the ways I used to greet myself on social media. Seriously. I'd open up Instagram and in those grainy camera pixels, all I could see were my blemishes, dry skin, and bags. I'd take pictures and immediately sift through all the filters.

I really felt ugly.

One time, I was in the back seat of my friend's car blurting out everything I wanted to change about myself. Meanwhile, everyone else was silent.

You ever have one of those moments, where you stop to actually hear yourself talking? That day, I did.

When I looked up from my phone, my friend was staring at me through the rear-view mirror. She was concerned. I could see it all over her face. I realized then, that she and the other women in the car, didn't make a habit of critiquing themselves every day. They also didn't pick themselves apart with their iPhones.

At that very moment, I decided to go back to therapy. Literally. Right there in the back seat of my friend's Mercedes. I couldn't be this person for the rest of my life.

My therapist told me I wasn't depressed. Yay! At least, not according to the clinical definition.

However, she did confirm that I needed to do some major work on my self-esteem.

"Duh, lady!" I thought. I was skeptical of her, her couch, and her recommendations, but I was even more determined to stick with these sessions.

Weeks passed and each time I walked into her office, more and more of *him* was shedding. I could tell and so could she.

One thing that helped tremendously was a journal she told me to buy. I almost ignored her advice, but once I had my hands on the actual book — I saw the value.

Each morning, thanks to the writing prompt in my new journal, I woke up and answered questions like these:

What's my mood?

What's today's prayer for myself?

What am I going to repeat to myself throughout the day?

Those questions were easy, but I struggled to answer the final one. *What am I going to do for myself today?*

"I'm going to work and then I'm going to come home, cook and then go to sleep," I thought.

I hadn't considered setting aside time for *me* in years…or maybe, ever.

So, I started small. I planned time to catch up on episodes of my favorite TV show or to read a new book. Then, I started to really get a kick out of it. I watched as the list of moments I planned for myself…grew.

1. Catch up on three episodes of my show
2. Read two chapters of my new book
3. Call my Dad
4. Take my hour-long break at the park
5. Write for 30 minutes uninterrupted
6. Go for a swim
7. Go to see A Wrinkle In Time
8. Shop for a coffee table
9. Make a new vision board
10. Try the new boba tea spot

The more I did this, the more I fell in love with my entire day. I had something to look forward to! The chapters in a new book felt so freeing. Taking a walk in the park gave me the energy to finish out my shift. I started to appreciate the small things.

I ignored phone calls during *my* time. I didn't answer texts. I immersed myself in family. I went to the movies alone. I envisioned how I wanted to decorate my house, without anyone else's opinion.

Then, out of nowhere, my heart started opening up to the idea of love. Up until that moment, I kept saying I wasn't interested. Remember that whole "I won't even consider marriage for another two to three years" comment? Well really, I was on a five to six-year plan. All of a sudden, I kind of wanted to go on a date.

One morning, I woke up to pray and write in the journal. During my routine, I had this very sarcastic thought.

"Man. Even if I had *someone*, what would I do with him?"

At first, I laughed. Then, I discerned that my thought was really rooted in negativity. It was as if my mind was telling me I was too damaged to go on a date — not get married, not exclusively date, just go on *a date*. That same voice questioned whether I'd know how to strike up a conversation with another human being.

Pre-therapy Jazmin would have just let that thought settle, but those sessions were paying off. Almost immediately, I caught myself.

My counselor taught me the art of finding alternatives. To combat any idea that might try to tear me down, I simply had to choose a greater perspective.

"What would I do with a man?" I thought. "I'd have fun. I'd make him laugh. I'm freaking hilarious!"

The answers to my own questions kept coming. So, I kept writing.

"I'd get dressed up and look fabulous. I'd ask great questions." I said out loud. "Can't strike up a conversation? That's not true. I interview people all the time! I get lost in other people's stories! I listen. I'm engaged in what they have to say. I could get anybody talking."

Then, I dropped my pen.

It's like I came to myself. All along, whenever I tried to talk to my Ex, he told me I was awkward and weird, but that wasn't true either.

I thought about all the people who have come on the show and told me repeatedly, *"I was so nervous, but you made it so easy to talk!"*

I scribbled that down.

My next thought was how my Ex always said I wasn't classy; like there was something wrong with wearing an off-the-shoulder top or a dress with a cutout.

Again. I knew this wasn't *true* — but he said it long enough, in an isolated space, and the crap became fact. My Ex had me out here losing my mind at the mall; freaking out about a high split or a deep-V.

Oddly enough, the day before this remarkable moment during my prayer time, a friend said she'd help me find a dress for an upcoming party.

"We just need to find something that's classic," she said while winking. "That's you. *Classic.*"

I wrote that in my journal too. All of it. Her expression. Her words. It was a direct contradiction to his foolish remarks.

Next, I remembered all those times he called me ugly. Of course, that was a lie as well!

Weeks before my morning of revelation, I was standing at the mic as the keynote speaker at a gala. Throughout my talk, I shared bits and pieces of this story; including some of the ludicrous things my Ex said about my appearance. I told the crowd how my Ex felt I wasn't pretty enough to be his wife.

"What?" One man whispered. "You are *beautiful*, girl!"

"Dude was crazy!" Another man yelled from the back.

Each word I wrote reminded me of how people all over the room chuckled from their seats. What my Ex told me was just insanely untrue!

I moved on to the next line in my journal. "*You're too dark.*"

I laughed thinking of how passionate my Ex was when those words left his lips. The level of self-hate deep within that man was unreal.

That's when I remembered my trip to IKEA. I was on a quest to find wall art when I stumbled into the store. After wandering for hours, a woman stopped me on my way out.

“I just had to tell you. Your skin is just *beautiful*,” she said softly. “Pretty, *brown* skin!”

Before I knew it, I had pages full of lies and the alternative *facts* (pun not intended) to dispel them.

I sat back breathing heavily over the pieces of paper.

It wasn't just the bottle of perfume. Everything this man ever said to me — from the moment he entered my life — was a lie.

OIL POUR

Before writing this book, I didn’t think I was equipped to tackle the issue of domestic violence. I thought my story lacked the number of punches to the face, bruised eyes, and bloody lips necessary to convey the severity of the problem. I was wrong.

Another abuse survivor, who suffered a major loss at the hands of her spouse, assured me of this. “The bruises?” she said. “Those heal fast...but the emotional stuff, the things they say to you and the way they get into your mind? That just keeps replaying over and over, and no one can see it.”

She was right. Any pain My Ex inflicted on my body went away, but his words? They were the toughest to shake. So, let’s talk about language and verbal abuse because it’s real and can easily go undetected.

What boundaries have you set for your significant other regarding how they speak to you? Write down those words or phrases that make you uncomfortable or feel disrespected. Refer to this list often.

Is there something your significant other (past or present) said about you that you’ve accepted as truth? What makes it fact?

Chapter 23: I Did The Best I Could

I won't share every detail of my therapy sessions, but one appointment, in particular, stands out among the rest. It was emotional and freeing; possibly as cathartic as writing this book. I hope my words can adequately describe the healing that took place.

From her wingback chair across the room, my therapist leaned in and handed me a laminated list.

"Choose the statement from the first column that best describes how you're feeling," she said.

I struggled to identify with anything on that paper. All of the statements were so negative!

I'm ugly.

I'm stupid.

I don't deserve love.

...and so on.

I scanned the list up and down, keeping in mind the clock was still ticking on our appointment.

Surely, I no longer felt ugly. I also no longer identified with stupidity. Everything written in the last chapter, alone, was enough to rid my heart of those emotions.

Minutes passed, and I still couldn't make up my mind! I was convinced I wasn't lying or sugarcoating.

"Okay, maybe when I've gone too long without an eyebrow threading I don't feel as beautiful," I thought. "but that's normal and fixable! That's not *me*."

I scanned the page once more and finally, found the statement that matched most:

I should've done something.

Just across from that phrase were another six words that seemed to contradict my choice:

I did the best I could.

My best? In my marriage? I *definitely* didn't feel that. In fact, nothing about our union made me proud. Getting married two days after the engagement, not having a real wedding or better yet, wedding photos? I always felt shame. Each time I remembered one of the gut-wrenching details in this book, guilt weighed me down.

To my surprise, this chapter of beating myself up was about to end.

EMDR is a psychological treatment that uses sound and light to help patients process traumatic events. My therapist suggested I try it.

"People say it's like five years' worth of therapy in one session," she said.

That was enough to convince me.

In my case, the abusive things my Ex said and did were the trauma. Before this moment, I viewed myself as his helpless victim. In my mind, I just stood there and let someone bully me for two years. I never fought back.

At my therapist's request, I put on a pair of headphones she'd given me, and almost immediately, I could hear these faint sounds in the distance. The intermittent static was calming as I listened to her instructions.

"Remember. You're in control. This is in the same vein as hypnosis but it's NOT hypnosis," she said. "You're in control. Always. Okay?"

I nodded and closed my eyes.

"Alright. Find your safe place," she said.

The mountains in Virginia.

I envisioned all the bright colors of the Fall leaves in the Shenandoah Valley. It was the most peaceful place I ever lived. I had a second thought to choose London, but it was too late.

Beep. Beep. Beep. Beep.

The sounds switched from one ear to the next and back; increasing in frequency. Then, from time to time, they seemed to slow down before ramping back up.

"Get a picture in your mind of that moment, that epic moment, you associate with feeling like you should've done more," she said. "Got it?"

There were so many moments. I struggled to choose just one. Instead, I situated the headphones a little better on my ears. They weren't tight enough.

"Just let your mind go to that place," she said.

I let out a deep sigh.

That time in the closet.

That's where my brain landed.

Then, the beeping started again.

At first, it was difficult to tune out the sound. There was a battle going on between those sharp vibrations and the image of me staring down my Ex. My closed eyes were switching from one side to the other; traveling with the sound.

I took a deep breath, and in the release, found a space where my thoughts and the beeping, could co-exist.

That day in the closet, my Ex told me I couldn't wear my white pencil skirt to a friend's baby shower. I was already running late and just needed to get out the door. I couldn't do that, though. He positioned himself in the doorway — seemingly letting me know I would have to fight to get past him. Once again, he felt my skirt was too tight.

It was not.

I remembered this situation like so many others.

"I just stood there," I thought.

I was so angry and tense, my fists started clenching into a tight ball as I sat on my therapist's couch.

"Just remember these things are like a train. They're passing you by," my therapist said. "If you can create some distance between you and them, do it. Put it up on…like a big screen at the theater. Remind, yourself. You're not *in* it."

So, on that imaginary theater screen, I watched this tragic scene; allowing my memories to fill in any gaps.

I pictured myself holding onto the theater railing like a Marvel fan, waiting patiently for any remaining post-credit scenes. From that distant position, I started to see things differently.

I *did* stare him down, and then, in a move of defiance, I lunged forward straight into his body. I was determined to wear what I wanted that day. Something in me must have said, "I'm going just the way I am!"

He retaliated by pushing me backward with all his strength. My clothes acted as reinforcement. Surely, without them, I would've fallen straight to the ground. My head likely would've hit the drywall.

"That's how I ended up on the ground," I thought. "Yeah. He pushed me, but I did something. I didn't just stand there."

I saw myself at that moment; the *real* me, acting on the big screen. I realized I wasn't weak.

I gave my Ex everything I had that day.

I did the best I could.

My mind quickly moved to the next scene — *the morning he dragged me across the carpet.*

I gulped before continuing. My therapist warned me this would be rough and she was right.

I remembered screaming at the top of my lungs as the carpet bristles scraped the surface of my skin. It was like he took a Brillo pad and scrubbed my entire left side — calf to armpit. I remembered trying, desperately, to hold on to a locked chest situated in the corner of our bedroom and then losing my grip. I remembered his words.

"Get the fuck out," he kept repeating. "Bitch!"

All these memories had replayed in my mind so many times, but I hadn't given much thought to what happened moments before.

Seeing your life on a big screen makes you ask questions, though. Like "How did I get there?" and "Why was he so angry?"

Well, I got up. That's the answer. I got up.

My Ex had this thing about staying in bed on Saturday mornings. It wasn't to talk or to watch a great TV show. I fully believe he enjoyed watching me suffer and squirm for hours. As I told him, I couldn't sleep past 7 o'clock.

If I were to go get water or tea and sit down to drink it on the couch, he'd come to find me. He always moved in silence. Each time, I didn't even know he was there, so I'd jump at the sound of his voice.

"What are you doing out here?" he'd ask.

"Ummm, just reading something on my phone," I'd say. "I needed something to drink."

My explanations were never enough. He knew I was afraid and pounced.

"Jaz, come back to bed. You know I don't like when you get up without telling me," he'd say. "If we're getting up, we're getting up together."

Our bedroom was a dungeon. I'd lay there for hours watching him sleep. If I even moved to grab my phone, he'd open one eye.

That morning, though — I got up. I pushed back the sheets, scooted my behind off the bed, and stood up. He jumped up too and went straight for the doorway, per usual. He dared me to try and leave the room.

With my eyes closed, I saw myself almost push past him. That's when the scuffle began. He knocked me down, first to the edge of the bed and then to the floor. I was on my back trying to free my wrists from his grasp.

If I didn't have any backbone, I would've been in that bed all day. Eventually, he yanked my arm hard and I lost control. He hauled me across the carpet, from the bedroom out to the kitchen. He didn't have to do that, but it didn't matter now. I survived.

I had to keep going. There were deeper wounds to heal. Some of these things were easy to dismiss on the surface, but in reality, they left gaping holes in my ability to trust. Like the time he refused to tell my father whether he'd protect me on our cruise to Mexico.

"Just make sure you're watching out for my daughter in that water," my Dad joked. He was halfway serious. I had already told my father we planned to snorkel.

"Oh, I know how to swim," my Ex responded.

"Well, I know *you* know how," my Dad explained. "She doesn't. Make sure you take care of my daughter."

"Yeah…I can swim," my Ex said in defiance.

Sitting in that chair, in my therapist's office, I wanted to strangle him. How freaking disrespectful and heartless could he be?

Either way, I agreed. *I did the best I could.*

I'm not just saying that to make myself feel better. After watching a few of these scenes play out, I realized that all those times my Ex was verbally abusive — his words literally shocked me.

I froze because his behavior was *that* abnormal, not because I'm stupid or an idiot.

I must have been thinking, "What kind of person says this stuff? Who paces back and forth when they talk? Who changes their mind after an hour of yelling, with spit forming on the sides of their mouth? Who just snaps out of their anger and asks for a kiss?"

I did the best I could in those moments.

I distanced myself. I stood across the room and watched. I prepared to protect myself should I need to.

Watching this footage on the imaginary big screen helped me to see, I had to forgive myself for what I didn't know back then.

On the way home from therapy, I cried in the car thinking about how I'd only ever received love from the men in my life. I wasn't used to this kind of treatment. Before my Ex, every man I knew had shown me kindness, generosity, chivalry, and care.

My dad? I was his little princess. In fact, I still am! He calls me "little one" even though I'm well into adulthood, and I'm fine with that. If people don't give you nicknames, they don't really love you!

I'm his *little one,* who he always rewarded with dates to Bob Evans for blueberry pancakes, just because.

His *little one,* who was driven cross-country to find the best college to make her dreams come true.

His *little one,* that he still picks up and carries to the car if she, jokingly, says she's too tired to make it.

I have pictures to prove it.

My uncles? They've essentially adopted me. They tell people I'm *their* daughter. They'd give me the world if they could.

My former pastor while growing up, Elder Lipford?

"*There goes my Jazz!*" He'd say whenever I did a great job in the Easter play or won a game at our Vacation Bible School picnic. I could always expect a warm hug on Wednesday night after Bible Study.

My ex-boyfriends weren't perfect — some cheated, others could just never mature — but they never talked down to me. Kindness, being showered with gifts, the effort to plan dates, biting their tongues when I got angry, being frustrated with me but choosing to just walk out of my dorm room or my apartment rather than go off on me? *That* was my norm.

I'd never been coached or trained on what abuse looked like in a relationship. It wasn't something I researched.

I'm not sure what class I was in during my four years at Michigan State, but I do remember a professor saying something that stuck with me.

"You can never be held accountable for something you haven't been taught."

That was true for this situation and will remain true for the rest of my life. *I did the best I could.* I can only be held responsible for what I knew to do at the time.

Kissing him.

"Ugh. Stop kissing me like that!" he once yelled.

As I remember, my Ex wanted to control the direction in which my tongue moved. Sitting there with my eyes closed, I remembered all of his bizarre instructions.

"Okay. Come close," he said.

Just as my lips were about to touch his, he threw me off by saying, "Now, slow down. SLOW DOWN!"

It was so forced and manipulated, I didn't even want to kiss him anymore.

"Softly," he said as our lips locked. "Okay. Now, tongue…TONGUE!"

I couldn't understand why he was yelling. Didn't he know that any commentary during an intimate moment was disturbing?

I nervously stuck out my tongue and connected with his. Then, he pulled back just enough to talk.

"Okay. Now move it softly," he said.

It was the strangest freaking thing I'd ever experienced. I cringed, but watching this on the imaginary screen made something click: *His actions* were odd, not mine.

Did anyone else prior to my marriage have any problem with the way I kissed?

No.

I wasn't odd. My behavior wasn't strange. *He was.*

I did the best I could with what I was working with!

Seconds later, an even better revelation manifested.

"Not only did I do the best I could," I thought. "He was in over his head. I was so freaking out of his league!"

"How are we doing?" my therapist asked.

"Ummm. Good?" I said.

"Where are you?" She asked.

"*Halloween.* I just remember him being weird."

"Okay. Take a deep breath…and just go with that, you're doing great," she said.

With my eyes closed, I saw us driving in his raggedy, old BMW. For some reason, he wanted to leave the $130,000 car parked at home that night. We had no plans on going out for the holiday, but in a rare moment of spontaneity, he agreed to do something fun.

"Let's just dress up and go get free Chipotle!" I said.

He didn't even know me. I love holidays! I go all out for Halloween. Learning to sew is still on my bucket list.

Why? So I can make my kids' awesome costumes. I'm dead serious. I'm totally going to be *that* mom.

We lacked the proper materials on such short notice, but we improvised, just to let loose. He dressed me and I dressed him. He wasn't having fun, though. I could tell.

He was silent as we ate, and any time I got excited about someone walking into the restaurant in a hilarious costume, he pretended to laugh; falling all over the table and slapping his knee. He was overcompensating.

As I watched the big screen, I felt like I saw him, the real *him*, for the first time.

He was out of his element. If it didn't involve salsa, teaching someone the Bible, or praise and worship — he didn't know how to operate. He just shut down.

This scene brought back an overwhelming amount of sadness; possibly more than the dragging or the pushing. He made Halloween boring. He wasn't engaged, at all.

His painfully-nervous state, at what any normal person would deem a fun, social event, was evident once again *when we went to a food and wine festival.*

"I totally forgot about this!" I thought as the beeping in my ears increased in volume

I was in heaven the night of the festival. The music! The food! Oh my god. It was delicious! But when I looked over at him, I remembered seeing the same awkward look on his face. He didn't know what to say or do. He even asked me that.

"What do we do here?"

"Well, we walk around, get samples and then they want you to score the restaurants," I said.

I really wanted to say, "What does it matter? We have tickets to eat all night! Bruh. Just enjoy!"

I was getting a wide-lens view of our entire relationship and I could finally see, he wasn't a fully-developed person. He couldn't deal with social situations. He didn't know how to respond. He couldn't just chill.

As I mentioned, he was, however, extremely jealous. He didn't like doing things I suggested or attending events where my local celebrity status opened doors.

It bothered him that I'd made progress toward my dreams. He couldn't stand the fact that I was going full-steam ahead, despite the abuse; checking off each goal, one at a time.

It irritated him when people stopped to say, "Oh! Jazmin! It's so nice to see you out and about! I'll be watching Monday!"

Those were the moments where the man with a doctorate degree felt small; like he could've disappeared. He was in competition with me.

"Wow. This is showing me so much," I thought while scooting back a little more on my therapist's couch.

I really did do the best I could.

I did my best to make him feel comfortable.

"You're so sweet," I'd say to viewers. "Thank you for watching. Did you meet my husband?"

I never left him out. I didn't want him behind me. I tried, desperately, to show him I wanted him beside me. If he couldn't realize that or if that wouldn't suffice — that wasn't my problem.

Next, I remembered something that still hurts to even write.

Missing the funeral for my best friend's mom.

My Ex said we didn't have any money and I didn't fight him. I was at the height of my mental breakdown and didn't want to create another blowup. I was trying to protect myself. I didn't know any better.

Not leaving sooner.

I didn't know I had the right to go. I felt alone. I thought no one in Florida would care. I didn't know people would take me in.

When he conned me out of the car.

I could scream. I saw the evil in his eyes, but I also saw…that *I did the best I could.*

That was a terrifying moment for me. He planned and executed that entire scheme, but days after, I started planning my escape. I left him less than three weeks later.

I also realized, there was nothing I could do about the car. It's gone but I got something new. There's no need to feel angry.

I did the best I could.

My head felt like it was swelling. The beeping was rapid, and my mind was processing so much. It felt like a buildup was forming in my temporal.

The time he called me "a terrible woman" for not fixing up our last apartment.

Days before this particular argument, he yelled at me for spending money on pots and pans. How was I supposed to know he wanted me to decorate? How the hell was I supposed to do that without any cash?

He wanted a mind reader.

I did the best I could.

Have *my* living spaces been decorated since leaving him? Yes. Just the way I like them! I'm not a terrible woman. He was confused and confusing.

"Okay. I think we'll stop here," she said. How do you feel?"

"Ummm…Good!" I responded.

"I want you to scan your body," she said. "I want you to go over every part of it and just repeat after me, *"I did the best I could."*

My throat.

All the lumps.

All the times I swallowed my pride and didn't retaliate.

Every time fear throbbed within that small space.

I did the best I could.

My chest.

The pressure of his two hands and the force of his muscles pushing me — the impact so strong I sometimes forgot to brace my fall.

Tail bone hurt.

Back hurt.

I did the best I could.

I could sense my body wanting to yell, "*You didn't protect me!*"

Exhale.

I did the best I could.

My arms that were dragged.

I did the best I could.

My neck that couldn't turn for days.

I did the best I could.

My eyes that, so often, swelled with tears.

I did the best I could.

My heart that broke — from loneliness and always being misunderstood.

I did the best I could.

"Okay. You can take the headphones off," she said.

"Well, I think you may need another one of these sessions. I'm not sure you worked through the entire image in your mind."

I was shocked by her words. I couldn't understand what she meant. As I opened my eyes and took off the headphones, I felt so…relieved! Everything made sense. I had an answer for all those questions I carried for so long.

I saw strength in myself for the first time in years. I saw guts. I saw determination. I saw a woman with the will to survive.

"On a scale from one to ten, how much do you identify with that statement, '*I should've done something?*'" she asked.

"I don't identify with it at all. I realized that I *did* do something," I said. "I'm not blaming myself for the violence. I'm just saying that there were plenty of times where I acted. I fought back. I spoke up. I held the keys. I wrestled my way free. I went to hang out with the friends he'd forbidden me to see. I didn't just sit there."

My therapist was shocked. I could see it all over her face.

"Wow. It seems like you really got clarity," she said

"Yeah, I did."

There was a pause. Not an awkward one. I knew our time was up, but I had to say one more thing.

"You know, it's kind of crazy because the last time I was here, you kept asking me if I was angry with him."

"Uh-huh…." she whispered while squinting her eyes.

"Well, it's funny because that same week I prayed about moving forward with this treatment and my pastor preached about the same thing," I said.

"He told us that God doesn't make us forget things, because then, we could forget Him. However, He does remove the pain and hurt of the moment."

She smiled.

"That's what you were saying? That after this session, I would remember being married but not the pain of each situation, right?"

"Yes. That's correct," she responded.

"See, what's interesting is that my pastor said the process was all about forgiveness," I explained. "You have to forgive that person for whatever they did to not remember the pain."

Her smile grew.

"It took me a few days, but I prayed again and in the middle of prayer, I just said it.

'I forgive *him*, God….and I forgive *myself*.'"

"That's good," she said.

I paused again. I was fighting back tears.

"Yeah. I just decided I wasn't going to walk around here acting like I haven't been harboring all of this anger and frustration toward him."

I suppose I wanted one last time to scream at him, as loud as I could; hurling all the awful things he ever said to me, right back at him. I wanted to make him feel my pain, but that's not how this works.

Forgiveness is sweet. It's the fragrance the violet leaves on the heel that crushed it. That's Mark Twain's definition.

Here's mine: It's letting go of the pain, not knowing if the person will ever pay for what they've done.

Chapter 24: The Forgiving Call

I looked up at my friend for that last bit of approval. I wanted her to tell me I was doing the right thing.

"I don't know what I'm going to say," I whimpered.

"Just say I forgive you and then, HANG UP!"

We both busted out laughing, thinking of how ridiculous that would be. Comic relief sure does the body good.

Sitting in her swivel desk chair, I dialed the ten digits I hadn't planned on ever seeing again. My friend's oscillating fan was blowing cold air directly onto my body. God knew I'd need a breeze. I was sweating.

The last time my Ex and I spoke was the day of the final divorce hearing. He was so chipper walking out of the elevator.

"Make sure you take care of yourself, Jaz!" he said.

Days before the hearing, when we met to close all of our joint accounts, he had stormed off from the bank.

"This chick!" he mumbled under his breath.

Now, as I listened to the phone ring, I really didn't know what to expect. I wasn't sure which version of my Ex I would encounter.

There was a huge chance he would rudely dismiss anything I had to say. I decided that possibility was just fine. This phone call wasn't about him. For weeks, I felt compelled to do this.

The phone rang…and rang….and rang. I started to think he wouldn't answer. My hour-long lunch break had seemingly been wasted.

Then, the ringing stopped. He *picked up.*

His voice sounded like I'd just interrupted some good sleep.

“Hi,” I whispered before clearing my throat. “Do you know who this is?”

A silence rested on either end of the phone.

“I have no clue,” he said.

That was fair. I'm sure I didn't sound the same. Plus, the number was random, and it had been a whole two years. Of course, he was clueless.

“Well, I just thought I’d ask,” I said, before pausing to continue. “I figured it might make this less awkward. This is Jazmin….Bailey.”

“JAZZ?!” He could barely get my name out of his mouth. He said it once more, losing what was left of his voice.

My phone call had knocked the wind out of him. In the background, I could hear a commotion; possibly him jumping out of bed.

“Yeah, it's me,” I said.

There was more silence before my Ex brought the lull in conversation to an end. He was sorting out his thoughts while talking.

“Umm, I didn't want to cut you off…I know I used to cut you off all the time…” he said. “How…how are you?”

“I'm good,” I responded.

I could hear him place his hand over his mouth in disbelief. He really couldn't believe we were on the phone. If I were honest, I couldn't believe it either. God knew, I never in a million years, planned to do this.

“Well, I just wanted to call and let you know I forgive you,” I said. It was short and sweet. Simple and to-the-point.

“Oh my God,” he said. “Jazz, *Thank You.* I know you don't have to do this, but thank you. I really appreciate that.”

“You're welcome,” I said calmly.

I meant it, but the words were still hard to swallow.

“Seriously. Thank you…How are you?” He asked again.

“I'm good.”

Your parents and sister?

"They're good."

"Work? I'm sure you're killing it…you know, Oprah and CNN!"

"Yeah…"

My voice trailed off. I wasn't here for flattery. I had said my peace and was ready to move on. Mission accomplished.

"Like I said, I know that you didn't have to do this…and I pray for you all the time. My mom prays for you that God heals you from all the things I did," he explained.

"Well…thank you," I said back.

I was surprised. Was that a partial-confession? I didn't even think I'd get *that* much.

"I know today, you calling to say this, that God's done that. You know? *Healed* you," he continued.

"Yeah..."

"Well, do you mind if I pray with you?" he asked.

I paused.

My first thought was "ABSOLUTELY NOT!" — but I opted for a softer letdown. My tone may have been gentler, but my decision was instantaneous. He was not praying for me!

We hung up a short time later after he wished me well.

"Nothing but God's best. His blessings on you the rest of your life," he said.

That was it.

Chapter closed.

No formal apology. No blow-up argument.

I simply forgave him and relieved myself of carrying that weight. It was no longer mine to carry. I wasn't a victim. I survived.

I wasn't in pain from his words. I knew and believed they were lies. I wasn't grieving. I was finally open to love again. I wasn't angry with myself. I *did the best I could* and believe I'm better because of it. What did I look like letting that weight hold me down?

I will say, that I'm human and even in the freedom of knowing I'd confronted my anger and resentment head-on, I thought once or twice "But God! Is he going to suffer…even just a little?"

Then, I thought about choosing the greater perspective. That process forces you to ask deeper questions. How would seeing him suffer positively impact *me*?

Would I even be able to witness this pain to gain the satisfaction I crave?

And if I could be a witness, would it be right for me to enjoy someone else's demise?

No, it would not…and it wouldn't bring any positivity into my life.

I sat at a red light on my way back to work and smiled. I was free as a bird.

Better yet, I am free.

Chapter 25: On Leaving

One time at the mall, when I was young and naive, I got suckered into a presentation for a car. I sat there, annoyed, staring at the salesman and his crooked teeth. He was trying to pressure me into an older model Nissan. I could see the dirt under his fingernails and the desperation in his pitch.

I'm not knocking a hard-working man, but I knew, if I were buying a car, I deserved better than this! I wasn't buying anything from this guy. Something in me screamed *"I don't belong here!"* and I got up and left.

That is literally the key to taking back your power. So many women have asked me how I finally found the strength to leave. You have to have the epiphany that *you don't belong in an abusive environment*—hopefully sooner, rather than later.

While married, I really didn't believe I deserved better than what my Ex had to offer. I *wanted* better, but that's not the same as knowing you deserve better! I also wanted better from *him.*

It's like demanding better service from a sleazy car salesman. This person makes a living by preying on the most vulnerable people looking for a deal.

He's not going to give you better! He can't give you better. Better doesn't exist in him! You have to wake up!

My Ex was trying to conform to what I needed, but the husband I got always fell short. He was exactly what he was capable of giving: rude, mean, critical, and angry. Those are the only traits he had to offer *me*, at least, consistently.

When the car salesman got a sense that he was losing his grip on my attention, he pulled out all the stops.

"Wait one second, Miss! I've got something for you!" he said frantically.

I was so annoyed. Seconds later, he brought back a dirty sheet of white paper with an *irresistible* offer: a refurbished smartwatch would be all mine! If only I surrendered all my personal information.

Ugh.

My Ex was the same. Flowers, candy, love notes, and fancy dinners were always presented — just when he felt like I was slipping away! They were all empty promises and I fell for them, more than once.

If you're in an abusive relationship and haven't had the epiphany yet, here's the moment you've been waiting for — YOU DESERVE BETTER!

I also want to address the Christian women who may be afraid that God will judge them for leaving. There's Bible for that!

Ephesians 5:25

25. Husbands, love your wives [seek the highest good for her and surround her with a caring, unselfish love], just as Christ also loved the church and gave Himself up for her.

Ask yourself: Does your husband love you as Christ loved the church? It's a very simple question.

How did Jesus love the church? He died for it. He laid himself down. He did what his body didn't want to do. He loved us. He cherished us.

He surrounded the church with care. He sought the highest good for her, even if it meant him harm.

That scripture freed me.

I had to ask myself:

Would Jesus push me?

Would Jesus shove me?

Would Jesus call me a bitch?

Would Jesus tell me I'm worthless?

Would Jesus threaten to leave me?

Would Jesus drag me?

Would Jesus ever be jealous of my success?

The answer is *no.* Jesus would never do any of that.

If your husband decides he's not going to fulfill his call in the relationship — to love you with Jesus' love — he's broken the agreement. Again, marriage is a legally binding contract. All of those behaviors I just described were a breach. I had every right to go.

The problem was, leaving scared me. I thought God would never have anything to do with me if I left, but that's just not true.

God didn't leave me!

Some may be wondering, "*but did she do everything she could?*"

I was certainly submitted to my Ex. I let him lead...to a fault.

Did I pray? Every morning. Every night. Constantly, I was looking into myself. Have I shown love today? Was there any other way I could've supported him?

Have I made this house peaceful, regardless of how I feel? Did I listen to what he had to say? Did I speak in *his* love language? Was I helpful or a hindrance to his success?

I had entire notebooks filled with Bible verses to pray over our relationship. I desperately wanted the words on the page to become my reality. I meditated on loving him and him loving me back.

I envisioned him accepting my embrace while saying to myself, "My husband is delicate with me! He enjoys my company!" and various other affirmations.

It didn't work in the time we were married and at some point, I decided I wasn't willing to wait and see if it would.

Part of my epiphany was realizing that while I *could* use my faith to see him change and finally love me, I didn't want to, and that was okay. To me, after all the fights, all the arguments, all the mean things said, *he* wasn't worth it.

That doesn't mean he's worthless. Surely not. It just means he wasn't worth any more of my time. Something in me screamed, "*I don't belong here!*"

I realized it was okay to let go…of him and the church I attended.

They were both were manipulative and controlling environments. Neither was a good fit for me, so I walked away.

Should you decide to do the same, it is important to have a plan. Every situation is different, and your abuser may not just let you walk away. The National Domestic Violence Hotline is open 24/7, year-round. Call them.

Also, while I felt compelled to call my Ex and verbally forgive him, that's often not a safe decision to make. Be smart and as I said, seek help before you leave.

National Domestic Violence Hotline:

1 (800) 799-7233

Chapter 26: On Quitting

To all my writers: There were so many moments I wanted to give up and not write this book. I would sit at coffee shops for hours and not come up with a *single* paragraph. I couldn't find the words, and I doubted if anyone wanted to read the story I had to share.

I cried. I broke down. I had multiple personal crises. It felt like the entire world was against me and I had so many questions swirling in my head:

Who will help me edit?

Who will take my cover photo?

What will I name it?

Is it good enough?

Catchy enough?

Does the whole idea make sense?

Am I going to make any of my money back?

Can I swear *and* talk about Jesus?

And, while we're on the subject of those lovely curse words. To anyone who was offended, I apologize.

I left them in the final copy because I thought it was time we do away with this idea that Christians are perfect and don't have flaws. I didn't want to censor myself and make another abuse victim think my experience didn't make me angry.

I didn't want to pretend. That wouldn't have been the genuine me or the real story. Simply said, people don't connect with fake.

Back to the book.

Sometimes I was so overwhelmed and so discouraged with the writing process, I wanted to say "Forget it. I can't do this. I don't even know if people need to hear all of this stuff! Why am I sharing all of my business?"

I was going through so many changes, emotional moments, and unearthing old memories, all at the same time. That part almost killed me!

But did I die? *No.* I had to fight the urge to quit!

I would sit in creative spaces — boba tea shops, bao restaurants, parks — and pretend to not wipe away tears. Customers walking by didn't know I had to force myself to reflect on old Facebook posts from my engagement. They had no idea I was reading old love letters from my Ex…but I was! Talk about pain!

Bishop T.D. Jakes once said, "you can't have great passion without great pain. Passion and pain are the wonder twins of purpose."

He was right. Every time I forced myself to shed a tear and keep typing, I won. Being reminded of my mistakes and my Ex's ruthlessness was uncomfortable. I thought I had put all those terrifying moments of my marriage behind me, but the wounds had to be reopened. It was my purpose. *That* was my oil.

I got my best content from looking through old photos, posts, and emails. Yes, forcing myself to get real with the details made me emotional, but it also made me a better writer. I couldn't hide behind words that didn't hold any weight. I wanted people to get the true story; not the flowery version.

That's why I couldn't quit. That's why I couldn't just go home and sleep after work.

Every day that you wake up and go after your purpose, you're going to be opposed. It's your job to look past the discouragement and difficulties. You cannot put your dream back on the shelf!

Writers, sometimes it won't even be about sleep.

Sometimes you'll be wide awake and unable to hit a creative groove. Fight! If you can't type, write with pen and paper. If you can't write, pull out your phone and record an audio file.

If you can't record anything, make a Pinterest board about your cover photo. The bottom line is: DO NOT QUIT!

Do not shut down your computer until you've accomplished something that moves you toward your destiny each day. Oh, and compliment yourself along the way.

You bought the Scrivener app? Yesssss! Tell yourself, "You go girl!"

Shoutout to Luvvie Ajayi for that tip! Scrivener saved my whole life. Out of convenience, I wrote the majority of this book on my iPhone. Don't let anyone or anything stop you. Tell yourself you can do this!

Acknowledgements

I have a long list of people to thank. Without them, this book would have never made it to print. Some inspired and coached me, others cheered me on and then, there were those who got their hands dirty on this project. To each of you: thank you from the bottom of my heart. I appreciate you more than you'll ever know:

Shakera Akins

Sherilyn Bennett

Natalie Black

Felichia Chivaughn

Angela Harrison

Alicia Hatcher

Tanae Howard

Jasmin Jordan

Dr. Keita Joy

Kevin & Kiki Morrison

Joyanne Panton

Sasha Perez-Loor

Natalie Pryor

Sierra Rainge

Journalism & Women's Symposium

About The Author

Jazmin Bailey is an author, speaker and Emmy Award-winning TV personality. Jazmin believes in the power of authenticity and shares her story of perseverance and faith on various platforms. She resides in Cleveland, Ohio. You can find and follow her @jazminmbailey on all social networks.

Made in the USA
Monee, IL
26 March 2021

63926778R00085